Ethical Dilemmas
in Church Leadership

"Here is a down-to-earth, up-to-the-minute manual on paths of wisdom for handling such crises as arise in every congregation sooner or later. It is a uniquely valuable must-read and must-discuss for pastors and lay leaders everywhere, and the sooner the better, for the next pastoral crisis may break tomorrow. So I beg you: order your copy at once."

J. I. Packer
Professor
Regent College

"In a time of such moral looseness and ethical nihilism as we face today, all of Christ's servants are pressed to the wall with problems and difficulties of a kind and to a degree we never thought possible a generation ago. Michael Milco has focused sharply, written clearly, and shared wisely and Scripturally. This is for all ministers of Christ and all lay people. It would be an excellent study-book for church boards and it has promise as a sprightly ancillary volume in courses in pastoral theology in training schools at all levels. We sense throughout the strong leading of the Holy Spirit through the Word as opened to us through his sensitive and probing servant."

David L. Larsen
Professor of Preaching Emeritus
Trinity Evangelical Divinity School

"Here is a book that puts ministry in a context that holds us accountable to standards that are clearly the key to effective leadership. This is a good read."

Joseph M. Stowell
President
Moody Bible Institute

"Michael has addressed the top critical, complex, and sensitive church leadership problem of our day. If you desire more precious time with our Lord, get this book and eliminate countless hours of debate."

Raleigh B. Washington
The Rock of Our Salvation Church
Chicago, Illinois

"Ethical issues are the cutting edge of church ministry practice today. The purpose of this book is to enable pastors to partner together through prayer, discussion, and encouragement in the area of ethical choices in ministry practice. Pastor Milco provides the issues, a process for decision making, ethical guidelines, biblical warrant, approaches to solutions, and conclusions for each issue.

Although the nine issues discussed and processed represent serious problems in the church, the real value of the book is its process for the resolution of ethical crises. Ministers will be well served by developing competencies in ethical decision making and not just finding solutions for the present problems they face in ministry."

James M. Grier
Vice President and Dean
Grand Rapids Baptist Seminary

ETHICAL DILEMMAS IN CHURCH LEADERSHIP

Case Studies in Biblical Decision Making

Michael R. Milco

kregel
PUBLICATIONS

Grand Rapids, MI 49501

Published by Kregel Publications, a division of Kregel, Inc., P.O. Box 2607, Grand Rapids, MI 49501.

Library of Congress Cataloging-in-Publication Data
Milco, Michael R.
    Ethical dilemmas in church leadership: case studies in biblical decision making / Michael R. Milco.
        p.   cm.
    Includes bibliographical references.
    1. Clergy—Professional ethics—Case studies.
2. Decision making (Ethics)—Case studies. 3. Christian leadership—Case studies. I. Title.
BV4011.5.M48   1997   241'.641—dc21   96-52011
                                                                                CIP

ISBN 978-0-8254-3197-5

Printed in the United States of America

5 6 7 8 9 / 12 11 10 09 08

*To my wife, Karen,
who loves God and inspires my thinking
and my devotion to the Lord.
She is, and will always be, my best friend.*

CONTENTS

ACKNOWLEDGMENTS

SPECIAL THANKS TO Dr. Mark Fackler of the Wheaton College Graduate School who gave me the idea for this book, encouraged me on, and has never stopped believing in me. Thanks, Mark.

I also want to thank Dennis Hillman and his staff at Kregel for making the publishing of this book such a good experience.

This book makes use of several case studies that have been previously published and are used here by permission. Unless specifically noted, all other cases are fictionalized accounts based upon the author's personal experience and research, and any resemblance to persons living or deceased is purely coincidental.

INTRODUCTION

As I REFLECT ON MY own life and ministry, I have discovered learning is a lifelong process. A steady diet of the Word, prayer, the continual reading of books, personal evaluation, and counsel from others helps me to stay focused. Our people need us as shepherds to stay sharp and fresh, but more importantly, *we* need to. This is my desire for writing this book. The Lord has spiritually and uniquely gifted pastors in order that the body of Christ might be fitted and joined together. He has also made us in different ways. Some of us are detail oriented, while others see the big picture; some are extroverts, others introverts; some have a left-brain emphasis, others a right-brain; and so on. Our passion for a particular theology bias finds us in differing camps on nonessentials and sometimes on the essentials of the faith. Our cultural backgrounds, theological training, ethnic diversity, and life experiences all converge in our decision-making processes.

Understanding the factors involved in making responsible ethical decisions takes time and practice. It reminds me of my older brother Ron, who is a trumpet player. While growing up in an apartment in Chicago, I had my share of listening to him practice hours on end every day until he got a certain piece down. Over the years, the sounds began to make sense to my ear, and eventually I appreciated his playing. He did several things to become a better trumpet player. First, he practiced daily, and, second, he kept his horn clean. I remember how he would fill up the bathtub with warm water, take the trumpet apart, and give it a bath. After it was cleaned to perfection, he dried it and oiled the valves before putting it back together. In so doing, his instrument was always at its best.

We have accepted God's call to be instruments He uses to proclaim the truth and further His kingdom. That is the wonder of His grace. Just stop for a moment and think about your life and ministry. Doesn't it make sense that we keep ourselves tuned to the factors that influence how ethical decisions are made in our ministries? Of course! The complexity of life challenges us to do so.

With the world changing faster than ever, today's pastor is expected to be steeped in more information than ever before. He is expected to wear many hats with a certain amount of expertise. The pastor knows what is expected of him.

- Live an exemplary life,
- Be available at all times to all people for all purposes,
- Lead the church to grow numerically,
- Balance wisdom with leadership and love,
- Teach people the deeper truths of the faith in ways that are readily applicable in all situations,
- Be a committed family man who demonstrates what it means to be the spiritual head of the family, a lover of one woman, and a positive role model for children,
- Keep pace with the latest trends and developments in church life;
- Build significant relationships with members of the congregation;
- Represent the church in the community,
- Grow spiritually,
- Run the church in a crisp, professional, businesslike manner without taking on a cold, calculating air.

The pressure on the pastor is enormous. It may be a privilege to lead God's people into a deeper relationship with Him. But, all too often, the privilege fits like a noose around the pastor's neck. By God's grace, he reasons, the slack in the rope has not been tightened.[1]

I remember my early years in the ministry when I just didn't have all the answers. I was young, with little experience and wisdom. Ministry was new for me. I didn't grow up as a pastor's kid or spend my free time during my teenage years hanging around the church. The dilemmas I faced in my early ministry left me feeling incompetent. I felt strongly about making the right decisions because I knew that making the wrong decisions wasn't like cutting a piece of lumber too short and just getting another one from the lumber yard. These were real people—God's people—entrusted to me!

Since those early days I have come to believe that the one area that stresses our lives more than theological tensions, worship styles, or other issues is how we reconcile ethical dilemmas while holding true to the Word of God. I recognized the stress back then but failed to wrestle with the issues. More often than not, I just answered each question in the same way for every dilemma. The following story illustrates my point.

A pastor was candidating at a local church. During the Sunday school hour he was asked to share with the fourth-grade-boys class. He asked the boys the following question:

"What is brown and furry, has a long tail, loves nuts, and climbs trees?"

Jimmy shot his arm into the air right after the pastor had finished asking the question.

"I know, I know the answer," he shouted.

"Tell us the answer, Jimmy," said the pastor.

"The answer is Jesus," he said with a slight pause, "but it sure sounds like a squirrel to me."

When it sounds like a squirrel, will we have the wisdom to say so? As pastors, in our hearts we feel the pain of our people. Disintegrating marriages, teenage pregnancies, financial failures, incest—you can name more, they all make their way into our offices. Some of them are too painful ever to forget. As the apostle John wrote, "The lust of the flesh, the lust of the eyes, and the boastful pride of life" (John 2:16 NASB) keep us all too aware of the struggles we face and the evil that invades the world. We know the Word is relevant and its principles are valid for everyday living, but there are times when those gut-wrenching situations demand more than a principle from a seminar or a quick and easy answer.

I want us to listen with wisdom to the cries of our parishioners and think about what should be done as we apply the principles of Scripture and consider all the variables that toss us around. At the same time, I want us to look in the mirror and remember that we too wrestle with our own humanity on a daily basis.

The questions I hope you will reflect on and honestly evaluate in your life are:

- How does my personality affect my decision-making process?
- What philosophy of ministry do I live by?
- Does the particular brand of theology I ascribe to lock me into a certain pattern?

For centuries people have wrestled with the ethical dilemmas of life. "The Greeks identified four chief or cardinal virtues: prudence, justice, courage, and temperance. Prudence is practical wisdom—that is, wisdom (not to be confused with intelligence or information) that leads to good choices and results in successful living. Justice centers on acts of fairness and honesty and the rule of law. Courage, also called fortitude, gives one the capacity to do what is right or necessary even in the face of adversity. And temperance is self-discipline, the ability to control one's impulses to do things that are gratifying in the short run but harmful in the long."[2]

The Pharisees tried to challenge Jesus with the question of taxes. Their cleverly disguised question had no clear-cut answer. Yet Jesus reminded them that man has a spiritual obligation as well as an earthly obligation. His answer appealed to their minds and spirits.

In 1 Corinthians 10:23–32 Paul addressed the dilemma of whether or not it was right to eat meat sacrificed to idols. He said, "For I am not seeking my own good but the good of many, so that they may be saved. Follow my example, as I follow the example of Christ" (10:33–11:1).

The Age of Enlightenment gave way to the birth of critical thinking, and the Reformation opened the way for Scripture to be the authority for life and practice. Man has come to the church as he wrestles with the complex challenges of life. "The savants of the eighteenth century recognized the need for morality, especially to keep the masses in line, and looked to the Judeo-Christian tradition to define moral behavior."[3]

The drift away from the biblical standards that once guided our nation has pushed us into a postmodern culture, requiring us to consider more factors when we make ethical decisions. The dilemmas we face pressure us to make wise choices.

My desire for this book is that it be used as a springboard for pastors of differing theological persuasions and denominations to come together in small groups to discuss issues and to encourage, pray for, and help one another in the challenging days ahead. I pray there may be a common ground for learning and partnering in the Gospel in this critical area of ethical decision making. I also hope this may be used where learning is exchanged to serve as an evangelistic bridge to counselors and others who help full-time ministers.

When we live our lives from the neck up, we live in an intellectual bubble with very little compassion. When we live our lives from the neck down, we are filled with a great amount of compassion, which sometimes blurs our ability to make wise choices. My prayer is that there might be a converging of our heads and hearts, for that is how God has made us. May God give us minds filled with wisdom and hearts overflowing with compassion as we move toward Christlikeness where He has called us.

As the days become increasingly filled with complex challenges, my experience has taught me to move slowly, become more keenly aware of potential trouble spots, and seek God's wisdom before making final decisions. "The study of ethics is a complex matter. We must proceed with a spirit of soberness and thoroughness, lest we satisfy ourselves with a simplistic approach to questions of great importance."[4]

CHAPTER ONE

ESTABLISHING ETHICAL FOUNDATIONS AND PERSPECTIVES

IN JULY OF 1981 a Gallup Poll was taken in which a cross section of Americans were asked how they rated persons of various occupations in regard to "honesty and ethical standards." Clergy were among a list of about thirty occupational categories. Sixty-three percent of those surveyed ranked clergy high or very high, 28 percent average, and only 6 percent low or very low (3 percent had no opinion).[1] This poll revealed the confidence churchgoers had in their ministers. In their minds the pastor had a special hotline to God. As a pastoral staff member in a world-renowned church, I am especially aware of this opinion. I frequently receive calls from different parts of the country regarding ethical dilemmas, from people in need of prayer, and from others seeking guidance for a difficult situation.

However, George Barna reported in 1992 that over the previous ten years, clergy had developed a tarnished image.

People make their views of the pastor known in a variety of ways. Sometimes those views are expressed in expectations or reviews of the pastor's performance. Sometimes they are communicated through people's lethargic response to calls for help or involvement in ministry. Sometimes people give evidence of their feelings by the manner in which they handle their most pressing problems.

Take for instance the confidence people have in the clergy during times of crisis. Only three out of ten adults admit that they would seek help from a minister during a difficult time. Recent Gallup surveys indicate that barely half the adult population has a great deal of confidence in the clergy. A recent Barna research survey found four out of five adults say they expect the clergy to live up to higher standards of behavior than they expect from other people.[2] The way we sometimes handle dilemmas is clearly supported by these findings.

Why the change? The growing awareness of pastoral indiscretion, possible abuse cases, and many other situations are causing some parishioners to doubt the wisdom of ministers. They want us to tell them God's will for a particular situation such as choosing a marriage partner or accepting a job transfer, yet they have trouble trusting us with their problems.

Most of the questions pastors deal with have to do with telling the truth in the largest sense: the obligation to be honest in our communications, how much truth to tell in differing circumstances, and the way in which the selecting and ordering of facts can distort truth telling. There is no way to grasp these issues apart from an understanding of basic ethical concepts and principles.[3] There were times when I wish I could have gone back to my seminary notes to find the formula that would give me the answer to a pressing problem I was facing. The dilemmas I struggled with were supposed to be everybody else's, not mine. You know, the ones you read about in books and shake your head over in disbelief. I was quickly learning I needed to find new options for making tough ethical decisions. Where was I to turn?

The pastorate today must face a multifaceted ethical maze. Confidential issues such as child abuse, incest, infidelity, AIDS, drug dependency, homosexuality, and financial crises often create uneasy tensions within the church. Most pastors are ill prepared to articulate a consistently Christian position because they do not have practice in professional ethics and are not always up-to-date on the legal parameters that could protect or indict them.

Today's minister is expected to understand the needs of every person in the congregation. We have discovered that our seminary and Bible school training does not prepare us for dealing with the ethical problems we encounter in ministry. The issues are tough because Scripture does not present clear and concise solutions for every human predicament. Combine difficult decision making with multiple personality types and differing theological and philosophical values, and the typical minister gropes for problem-solving options consistent with his training in theology and Bible.

How do ministers, denominational boards, and mission organizations confront and solve dilemmas in ministerial ethics? When confronted with ethical decisions, we usually do not stop to examine our methods of reasoning. A predominant mode of reasoning persists. The late journalist Edward R. Murrow was right when he said many of our convictions are just the rearranging of other people's prejudices.

During my first five years in ministry, I was the pastor of a small rural church in the Midwest. One Sunday afternoon I received a telephone call that challenged my thinking and exposed me to the ugliness of life and the sinfulness of people. A key member of my church had been indicted on first- and second-degree charges of child molestation. He was a charter member, family man, and for a time a deacon in the church. What should I do? How would I administer the love of Christ and preserve the integrity of the Gospel? Where should I strike the balance between maintaining the purity of the church and keeping the issue confidential? Would I handle the biblical text accurately in communicating the options? What process or framework could I work from? Whom should I tell? How would this affect the community of believers? These demanding questions forced me to think and pray harder than at any other time in my career as a pastor.

Not long after, I was called by an attorney to answer questions concerning a parishioner who had been indicted for another crime. I felt intimidated and fearful of what would become of my knowledge. Sure enough, the attorney's written report did not reflect the attitude I had tried to portray of the parishioner. I felt betrayed, and so did my parishioner.

Out of these experiences I felt the need for the development of case studies in pastoral ethics in order that we as pastors may understand (1) the tensions between biblical ethics and ministry, (2) the meaningful responsibility that must be distributed among those involved, and (3) the options for communicating these delicate situations with integrity toward the parties involved.

My purpose in writing is not to articulate a particular biblical ethic, for there are many fine works available that shed light and understanding on this area of theology. My aim is to assist church leaders in the decision-making process that affects the body of Christ.

> The enduring marks of biblical ethics are its foundation, in relationship with God; its objective, imposed obligation to obedience; its appeal, to the deepest in man; its down-to-earth social relevance; and its capacity for continual adaptation and development.[4]

Since the fall of 1992, when I joined the staff of the Moody Church in Chicago as pastor of families, the challenges have continued with even greater complexity. Urban ministry constantly has prodded me to articulate a framework of ethical decision making.

The need for considering how ministers communicate is made even more evident in an article that appeared in *Christianity Today* titled "Conduct Unbecoming a Preacher."

> Both Fortune and Norris Smith, a consultant with the (Southern) Baptist Sunday School board, point to a lack of accountability and clear professional guidelines among individual pastors as contributors to ethical misdeeds. Smith, a specialist in the area of forced termination of Southern Baptist pastors, conducted a study

revealing "immorality" as a leading cause of their dismissals, *second only to lack or abuse of communication* [italics mine].[5]

Ministers today are under tremendous stress. Studies have shown the greater the stress the less capacity to make sound judgments. As a result, many of our colleagues have fallen from grace or walked away from the ministry. "Plans fail for lack of counsel, but with many advisers they succeed" (Prov. 15:22).

Here are some typical cases. A couple attending the Moody Church adopts a child with AIDS. Pastor Erwin Lutzer challenges his congregation to be Christlike in their actions. The medical condition of the child comes under discussion by the church board and Christian Education committee, who prayerfully respond with the following public statement: "The boy is not allowed to attend Sunday school at the church at this time." What are the legal ramifications of such a statement? How was this communicated to the Moody Church congregation? What framework did the leadership use to make the decision? What levels of confidentiality were observed or violated?

Several days later, due to media attention, the statement is retracted with clarification. The boy is allowed to attend Sunday school at the Moody Church.

In another city, at another time, a member at Faith Baptist Church contracts the AIDS virus. The pastor feels compelled to tell the congregation the truth about the man's sickness. After a period of time, the congregation rallies around the man in prayer. Eventually the man dies but his struggle has brought the church closer together.

A large metropolitan church is shocked with the news that its senior pastor is resigning because of inappropriate sexual conduct. The church board wrestles with questions regarding the degree of discipline, who should be informed, and the reason for the pastor's resignation. How much of the truth needs to be revealed? Should the board attempt to quiet the situation? Did they integrate an ethical approach in communicating this situation? What other alternatives could there have been?

Elsewhere, a former pastor is nominated as an elder in the church. The nominating committee agrees that the nominee would make an excellent choice. That week, his wife calls the pastor disclosing information about her husband that would disqualify him from being nominated. How much does he tell the nominating committee? Would it be in the best interest for the nominating committee to know? Should the pastor call the church the nominee previously pastored?

My goal is to establish the different types of ethical dilemmas, through case studies, that pastors identify as the most difficult situations in their daily ministries. Most pastors with experience will be able to identify with these cases.

Creative analysis involves several clear steps. To understand the process more clearly, I have chosen to illustrate the decision-making process by using what I will introduce as the Decision-Making Tower.[6]

Dr. Ralph Potter of the Harvard Divinity School outlines four elements of ethical decision making that can be adopted for addressing dilemmas.[7] By using the Decision-Making Tower, one can rethink ethical dilemmas that seem to perplex pastors. This framework will give pastors a tool they can use when difficult ethical questions arise. The following diagram outlines the four principle components of the Decision-Making Tower (see fig. 1.1).

THE DECISION-MAKING TOWER

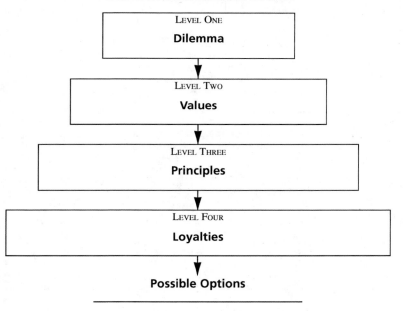

Figure 1.1

Any single decision in the pastorate revolves around defining the issue, personal values, a working principle (your personal brand of theology or philosophy), and loyalties. These become the components for responsible decision making. Not only our personal dynamics but our different personality types create the possibility for conflicts and increased stress. These different personalities, values, and ethical principles are the reasons why there is such a variety of decisions within the pastoral community. One pastor might argue for the love of Christ to supersede unethical behavior, while another holds fast to the principles of moral absolutes. With each case we pray hard, hoping to make the right choice, but seldom stop to examine our method of reasoning or consider other alternatives before making our final decision.

The Decision-Making Tower can help guide us systematically through the cases presented as well as those you will encounter in the pastorate. Based on the Decision-Making Tower, conclusions are morally justified by demonstrating clearly that an ethical perspective shaped the final decision. In this regard, we search the Word, our wills, and our emotions as we make decisions that impact God's people.

Let's walk our way through this useful tool in order to better understand the elements of each level. Looking at the first two levels of the Decision-Making Tower, we begin by articulating the case at hand and discerning what personal values shape our understanding and attitudes (see fig. 1.2).

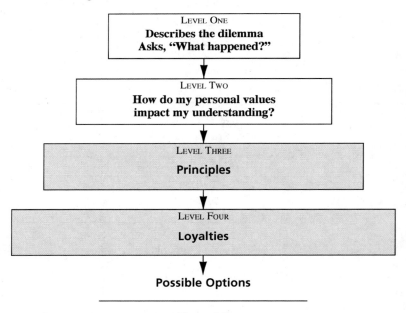

Figure 1.2

Level one can be best described as *defining the situation*. A church discovers, for instance, that its Sunday school superintendent has been taking money from the Sunday school's offerings. No one is sure how long it has been taking place or how much has been stolen. The situation presents a complex dilemma to the church board. The superintendent is the brother of one of the elders of the church. Should they confront the superintendent on the matter and possibly cause a split in the church?

Or should they just ask him to resign by citing other reasons without revealing the real reason to the congregation? In a closed-door meeting, the elders are split on their decision.

Using the Decision-Making Tower, the pastor has the opportunity to write down and rethink the dilemma at hand. In so doing he is able to understand some of the principle elements involved. An honest evaluation gives him the opportunity to reflect on his own values and the values of others.

As we shift our focus into level two, the pastor's own personal history or legacy is more clearly understood. Level two might best be described as *defining what I think is important to accomplish*. Sometimes the pastor is undoubtedly making a decision solely on the basis of his values or how he feels at this time in his life. Our values are important to us. To value something means we consider it desirable.[8] What type of values shape the decision-making process? Some people place a high priority on aesthetic values (harmony or pleasure), cultural values (hard work, frugality), moral values (peacefulness, truthfulness), professional values (innovation, creativity), or ethnic values. As pastors we often transfer our personal biases to a given situation without even realizing it. Our values reflect what's important to us. By working through the Decision-Making Tower we are able to concentrate on each part of the whole without mixing unwanted personal baggage into the situation. As we do this kind of analysis we can begin to understand how the different components in our reasoning influence the outcome.

Take the example of Rehoboam in 1 Kings 12. After Solomon died, the responsibility of leadership fell on Rehoboam. His most critical decision eventually split the kingdom. The subject of taxes came to bear on the king. What would he do? He sought the counsel of older, wiser men, who encouraged him not to place heavier taxes on the people. He also sought the counsel of younger, less mature men, those with whom he had grown up, who encouraged him to establish his authority by placing heavy taxes on the people. The younger men valued power and pride. They were insensitive to the people, and when Rehoboam took their advice, the nation of Israel split and never recovered. The influence of our personal values makes a greater difference than we realize.

As we move through the Decision-Making Tower, levels three and four give the decision maker the flexibility to wrestle with his theology, personality, philosophy, and loyalties as they relate to the situation and his own internal bias (see fig. 1.3).

Level three *defines your theological framework*. It reveals who you have been influenced by in life. Are you Catholic, Protestant, Calvinist, Armenian, dispensationalist, Reformed, liberal, conservative, or fundamentalist? Is your life guided by the concepts or principles of a noted author, speaker, or mentor?

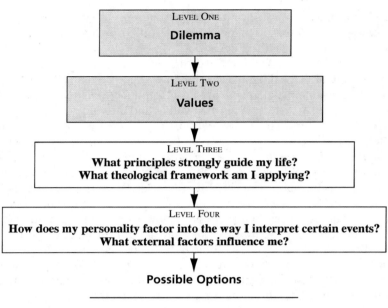

Figure 1.3

Have you come to an understanding of your personality style? Are you an introvert or an extrovert, a visionary or a manager?

Level four *defines the impact of your personality* on the dilemma. Reflecting on the disciples, we discover how their personalities impacted their actions and faith. Luke, for example was quiet and warm, a genuine optimist. Matthew was a problem solver, less outspoken than the others.[9] By looking at the situation from a different perspective, we gain a greater understanding of the core elements that shape our decision.

Also, in level four the decision makers wrestle with external factors that influence the ultimate choice. Level four *defines loyalties.* Consider your best friend, who is also in ministry, confessing to you that he has had an extramarital affair. It was a one-night stand that now threatens to swallow up his ministry and devastate his wife and children. What are your options? Your loyalties to him as a friend leave you with sleepless nights. Choosing your loyalties is an extremely significant step in the decision-making process.

Consider the relationship David and Jonathan had while Saul sought David's life. Jonathan repeatedly faced the tension between his loyalty to David and his relationship to his father.

My desire is that we consciously consider each level in the Decision-Making Tower in order to understand the dynamics in the decision-making process. In addition to considering each level carefully, the Decision-Making

Tower must be viewed as an organic whole, a flow of elements that continually interacts among the four levels. By understanding this interaction we realize there are no priorities to the different levels. The only two constants are the dilemma and the decision, while our principles, values, and loyalties are synthesized in the process. As a result, working through the Decision-Making Tower, in prayer, helps us as pastors gain more confidence when we are faced with ethical dilemmas beyond our experience.

To begin, I want to expand on level three of the tower and outline some ethical perspectives that will establish a foundation for guiding us through the Decision-Making Tower. Throughout history people have approached ethical decision making in various ways. Two primary discussions have been in the areas of culture and history and their influence on people and society. These perspectives flow out of external experiences of the world around us and the internal, personal understanding of our worldview. These ethical perspectives represent some of the variables that impact our decision making.

Why should we consider ethical systems that may not have biblical support? They are representative of our intellect, passions, theology, and personalities that consciously and unconsciously make up our decisions. Our biblical, cultural, and historical perspectives are like glasses through which we view the world. No one has 20/20 vision, although some may feel they see through the glasses more clearly than others. You may feel very comfortable in your approach, or you may be searching for options. Readers acquainted with other principles are encouraged to integrate them. The following perspectives are intended to help pastors articulate and understand some of the dilemmas we face in the pastorate today.

Many who love God have found strength and guidance in the Judeo-Christian love ethic, which has its roots not only in Jesus' life but in the words written in Matthew's gospel. "'Love the Lord your God with all your heart and with all your soul and with all your mind.' This is the first and greatest commandment. And the second is like it: 'Love your neighbor as yourself.' All the Law and the Prophets hang on these two commandments" (Matt. 22:37–40).

Our example from Scripture means that love is a sacrificial desire to seek the best interests of others by giving of ourselves so that good might be brought about in others. Our Lord displayed an unconditional love that was not self-seeking but sacrificing, distinct from personal gain, that paid the highest price, His life, in exchange for ours (Philippians 2).

In the course of church history, this Christian ethic based on instructed love has suffered from constant twisting and warping in every possible direction. That is, some have so severely warped the basic love ethic of the Bible that they have really moved outside the realm of what can rightly be called Christian.[10]

In considering the Judeo-Christian ethic, some people unconsciously have allowed "viruses" to make their way into the love Christ displayed to His disciples and followers. This is a list of some of the misinterpretations of the Judeo-Christian love ethic.

1. *Experientialism.* Its essence is to make religious practices or one's own Christian experience the central focus. In the Bible, the focus of the life of faith is always on God and, in a secondary sense, our relationship with others. Experientialism shackles immature believers because they view maturity through their own personal experience. This happens in the church when a particular spiritual experience is evident in one denomination or local church and not another. As a result, classism permeates the Christian community.

2. *Legalism.* Rules divorced from love lead to hardness and an inability to live up to the very rules recognized in the mind. Paul addressed this problem in his letter to the Galatians. The Judaizers were living out their Christianity by an obedience to a rigorous set of rules. When legalism is evident in the church and in the pastor, the decision-making process becomes hard and cold. The expression of love and compassion takes a backseat to formulated rules.

3. *Antinomianism.* The core teaching of antinomianism is that we love God and do what the heart wants rather than follow rules. The misconception is that if we love God we will inevitably do what is right. This reduces Christian love to a series of acts. The problem is that our love is never perfect; our actions, therefore, may stem from motivations other than love.

4. *Pharisaism.* A pharisaical character or attitude selects particular applications of love or virtues and judges life according to them. As a result, our attitudes toward others as seen through the Judeo-Christian ethic become condescending and judgmental.

The Judeo-Christian ethic requires us to act in love. The foundation of who we are as Christians is based on love and forgiveness. How this is applied in ethical dilemmas means that we review each situation and approach it with much prayer and wisdom.[11] Even our Lord balanced His unconditional love with justice. As much as we try to imitate God's love, each dilemma forces us to regulate how it is dispensed.

Throughout history people have searched for a philosophical model to guide them through ethically hazy questions. Some have been guided by Kant's categorical imperative of truth telling: "Act as if the maxim of the action were to become by thy will a universal law of nature."[12]

The statement has been made: "Truth telling is far better than peacekeeping." If one were to sum up the basic premise of Immanuel Kant it would have to be in this axiom. For Kant, the universal truth that right is right and wrong is wrong applies no matter what the consequences.

If we unequivocally adopt this premise as believers, especially those of us in church leadership, then decision making is not considered on an individual basis but on sweeping truths that must be obeyed regardless of socially accepted norms and standards. "Or putting it another way, a moral principle must be such that a man can will that all men, including himself, should act upon it."[13]

According to Kant, the litmus test of consistency is the core of fundamental moral law. If, for example, a minister is confronted with the dilemma of divorce between two Christians, outside of the biblical precedent, then the divorce is always wrong. The principle is binding upon everyone because within God's design there is an inborn conscience of truth telling that must be obeyed.

Kant's categorical imperative becomes especially difficult in the areas of discipline and confidentiality in the ministerial arena. As we consider the various case studies on the following pages, we'll see Kant's principle becoming for some a difficult tension in relationship to personal hermeneutics and theological preference. For others, Kant's axiom becomes a blanket for confirming theological beliefs.

Consider the church nominating committee that is split over the decision to accept a member as a potential deacon because he was divorced ten years earlier before he was a believer. Three members of the nominating committee hold firmly to the verse in 1 Timothy, "A deacon is to be the husband of one wife." The others consider the case individually and show compassion. If the person had been considered the year before with different people on the committee he would be serving as a deacon.

Or consider this problem posed to a class of clergy members:

> A husband and wife are interned in a concentration camp. They are housed in separate quarters with no communication between them. A guard approaches the wife and demands that she have sexual intercourse with him. She refuses. The guard then declares that unless the woman submits to his overtures, he will have her husband shot. The woman submits. When the camp is liberated and the husband learns of his wife's behavior, he sues her for divorce on the grounds of adultery.

When the clergy were asked, "Would you grant the man a divorce on the ground of adultery?" all twenty in the class answered yes. Even though they understood the extenuating circumstances, the fact remained that the wife's behavior was immoral.[14] Those who interpret life through Kant's principle, with no room for grace, will waste little time agonizing over personal dilemmas in making decisions but will spend a lot of energy persuading those who see things from a different perspective.

Still others have found comfort and stability in the writings of John Stuart Mill, who has given us the greatest-good principle: The greatest good for the greatest number of people should be the goal and standard of conduct of the individual. When this is practiced, the scales of pleasure and pain are tipped in favor of the good of all humankind. From the believer's perspective, this would be the greatest good for the body of Christ in relationship to obedience to the Word.

While this principle seems rather straight forward, it's actual application can become complex. Consider the problems one faces in trying to apply this principle to biblical events.

As the Israelites traveled in the wilderness toward the Promised Land, for most of them, their attitude would have to be characterized by murmuring and grumbling. Those that were stiff-necked and blatantly disobedient to Moses and Aaron were severely judged by God. In Exodus 32, after Moses descended from Mount Sinai, he finds the people dancing around a golden calf. The Scripture says "his anger burned." Realizing the people had committed a great sin, he says to the Levites, "This is what the LORD, the God of Israel, says: 'Each man strap a sword to his side. Go back and forth through the camp from one end to the other, killing his brother, friend, and neighbor.'" This was only the beginning of forty years of wandering in order that those who did not trust God would die without entering the land flowing with milk and honey.

Nehemiah made sweeping reforms. Today we might think they were cruel and insensitive. We read in Nehemiah 13:23–26:

> Moreover, in those days I saw men of Judah who had married women from Ashdod, Ammon and Moab. Half of their children spoke the language of Ashdod or the language of one of the other peoples, and did not know how to speak the language of Judah. I rebuked them and called curses down on them. I beat some of the men and pulled out their hair. I made them take an oath in God's name and said: "You are not to give your daughters in marriage to their sons, nor are you to take their daughters in marriage for your sons or for yourselves. Was it not because of marriages like these that Solomon king of Israel sinned?"

As a result of his reforms, he sent away the foreign wives and husbands married to Israelites and children who were of foreign descent. Nehemiah was seeking the greatest good for the nation of Israel after coming out of exile. He was a student of the Word and realized that in order for their greatest happiness to be achieved, they must find favor with God by obeying His Law. This meant that some would have to suffer the consequences of their disobedience.

This principle couldn't be more evident than in the life of Jonah, who was thrown overboard by the sailors so that their ship might not sink. Jonah 1:12 says, "Pick me up and throw me into the sea . . . and it will become calm. I know it is my fault that this great storm has come upon you."

Even Paul, in chapter 5 of his first letter to the church at Corinth, instructed the church to expel an immoral brother, "so that the sinful nature may be destroyed and his spirit saved on the day of the Lord" (v. 5).

Although we don't live in those times and justice is dispensed in different ways, the scenes have changed little with the times. Our focus for the church, as Paul describes in Ephesians 4, is still to build up and equip the saints to do the work of the ministry. In your church there may come a day when a child or an adult is diagnosed as HIV positive. How would Mill's principle apply in relationship to the safety of present-day Sunday schools, megachurch children's programs, or church intramural sporting events? How can we balance all the elements in relationship to the larger body of Christ? How would a church board apply Mill's principle when a pastor resigns because of a psychological breakdown or when a nationally recognized pastor gets divorced or falls prey to infidelity?

As we sift Mill's principle through the teachings of Scripture, we immediately recognize that families will get hurt, marriage engagements will be broken, and some will have to come to grips with how they are living their lives and how their lives impact the church.

Unfortunately, our decision-making processes are strongly influenced by social pressures, ethical norms, our desire to be liked, and cultural bias. It is, therefore, so important for us as ministers to understand all the dynamics that forge our decisions as we work to resolve the conflicts in ministry. In many instances, there are more than ethical principles at stake: dreams, hopes, futures, families, and people's lives all hinge, at times, on the words of the few and persuasive. As we think back to the Decision-Making Tower, we see that our theology, personalities, and principles for living influence the decisions we make.

Many other influences affect our ability to make right decisions. From a historical perspective, we can understand how our *culture* has influenced recent generations. Looking back over the past four decades, one notices pronounced trends in America. One cultural perspective influencing the Christian community in this century is the notion of Western individualism—the "take care of number one" attitude. For some this mind-set has become their defense mechanism, for others a lifestyle. Regardless, the church today is faced with this Goliath that can only be slain by the Spirit of God working through the people of God.

As we look at current events through the lens of Christ's teachings and the principles of Scripture, the need for security and hope scream out. In a day of cultural relativism we don't have to be in ministry too long to confront the materialism of the "baby boomer" who is approaching the age of fifty and is scrambling to save for retirement. The music of the sixties and seventies, the influence and themes of Hollywood, accompanied by the fractured family, all converge to produce a generation that seeks to satisfy itself.

To live for the moment is the prevailing passion—to live for yourself, not for your predecessors or for your posterity. We are fast losing the sense of historical continuity, the sense of belonging to a succession of generations originating in the past and stretching into the future. It is the waning of the sense of historical time—in particular, the erosion of any strong concern for posterity—that distinguishes the spiritual crisis of the seventies from earlier outbreaks of millenarian religion, to which it bears a superficial resemblance.[15]

On the other hand, Generation X maintains a less materialistic attitude than do the boomers. This is a generation looking to make a statement. They challenge authority and look to the church for more authenticity in relationship to the struggles of the day. Theirs is a generation of diminishing expectations. The Protestant virtues no longer excite enthusiasm—advertising undermines the horrors of indebtedness, exhorting the consumer to buy now and pay later. As the future becomes menacing and uncertain, only fools put off until tomorrow the fun they can have today. A profound shift in our sense of time has transformed work habits, values, and the definition of success.[16]

These two generations represent the church of today and the church of tomorrow. With their differing values and perspectives, the church needs to be called back to the claims of Christ and His deeds. In a day when instant gratification is the norm and many are trying to make a statement, what are our priorities? Are we contemplating eternal values and rewards as we teach and challenge our people to be change agents for the kingdom? Our challenge is to see through these myths and the absorption in self.

Facing difficulties in ministry forces us to consider the cultural influences of the day. It can be easy for us to succumb to the mind-set of Western individualism even in our ministries. Our own pride, jealousy, envy, and self-worth can create a callous coating that prevents us from seeking the advice, help, and prayer of wise counsel. As we peel off the veneer and we model Christlikeness, it will impact the decision-making process. Let us pray the transformation process will be an example to the flock we shepherd.

Consider the decision to accept a large donation from a particular member of the church for the development of a ministry that is not exactly in line with the vision of the church. The church needs the money, but if it accepts this gift it will be strongly influenced by the giver to grow using the methods of big business—like the giver's business. The church would feel that marketplace savvy is necessary for church growth, until eventually business know-how would supersede the place of the Holy Spirit or the body of Christ.

As we have witnessed throughout history, God grows His church in spite of us and in ways that sometimes appear to be a mystery. I'm sure in your ministry you have experienced your own examples. One thing we know for sure, as recorded in Scripture, it is the Spirit of God who brings people to the Savior.

Another complication in decision making is the *conscience*. In the decision-making process, the conscience ethic is prevalent, and our responsibility is to understand how God has wired us. The commandments of God are eternal, but to obey them we must first appropriate them internally. The organ of such internalization has been classically called the conscience. Some describe this nebulous inner voice as the voice of God within. The conscience is a mysterious part of a person's inner being. Within the conscience, in a secret, hidden recess—so hidden that at times it functions without our being immediately aware of it—lies the personality. Personality and personality types help shape our decisions.[17]

I remember, during my preconversion years, constantly hearing 2 Corinthians 5:17: "Therefore if any one is in Christ, he is a new creature, behold, the old has passed away, all things have become new" (NASB). My understanding of the Christian life was similar to going through a car wash. Before you ask Christ into your life you are dirty, after salvation you are clean through and through. While this is true positionally, experientially I still lived with my personal God-endowed circuitry.

The apostle Paul is a good example of this. Prior to his conversion experience, he was zealous for the advance of Judaism, even going so far as to lead the attack against the early church. After the Damascus road experience and his subsequent discipleship, he was still wired the same way. How did God change Paul? As I have faced dilemmas in the ministry and counseled others, the unspoken issue for many seems to be, "Can God really change me?"

Absolutely! But don't set your sights so low that you define your possibilities by merely natural standards. The starting point is this: You cannot begin to understand your full potential outside of a relationship with God, who has endowed you with all your traits and abilities.[18] I believe God not only transforms us spiritually but He also changes us as persons as we become students of ourselves.

In 1983 when I first began my ministry, I was clueless as to how God had wired me. Fresh out of seminary, I quickly learned pastoring was more than preaching and teaching. I bumped along by God's grace, developing my preaching legs but not confident when my board disagreed on issues that in my mind were clear. Only later, after I returned to school to pursue further graduate studies, did I begin to understand who I was in relationship to who they were.

In the last decade much emphasis has been placed on the personality profiles of those in leadership positions. In particular, many ministers have succumbed to the executive pressure of understanding themselves in relationship to their role as a shepherd of the flock. The influence of modernity and marketplace management has revealed itself in the decision-making process. Team-building and new leadership styles have in some ways been a healthy shift away from the omnicompetent pastor who attempts to process and formulate difficult ethical decisions without the support or input from others.

In the same way our theology or philosophy shapes and determines our judgments, so do the personalities of those in the decision-making process. Just as we are students of others, we need to become students of ourselves. Differences abound in all of us, but too often we conclude that those whose behavior is different from us manifest deviant, dysfunctional, or irrational behavior. Unconsciously, the goal is to surround ourselves in ministry with people just like us. When this occurs, the decision-making process becomes a pooling of similar ignorance.

Paul, in Romans 12:1–2, encouraged the believers to be transformed by the renewing of their minds. Yet, deeply ingrained within us is God's design of how He wired us. The best way to understand ourselves is to take a temperament assessment sorter.

The exercise below is designed to help you understand the meaning of the four preference scales (orientation, perception, decision making, and lifestyle) of the Myers-Briggs Personality Type Theory. There are no right or wrong answers.

Orientation. Is your life mostly oriented toward things going on outside yourself (Extroversion-E), or does your attention gravitate more naturally to your own thoughts and musings whenever possible (Introversion-I)?

Perception. Do you rely on and develop more fully your capacity to use your five senses (Sensing-S), or do you prefer to tap into your inner sense (Intuition-N) for information about life?

Decision making. Do you put more stock in logical analysis and objective, impersonal, rational thought (Thinking-T) in your decision-making process? Or do you ultimately put more weight upon your subjective evaluation of the situation (Feeling-F)?

Lifestyle. Do you enjoy approaching life from an ordered and structured standpoint (Judging-J) or in an open, spontaneous manner (Perception-P)?

Although each of us use all eight options in the course of everyday life, we usually prefer one over the other in each set.

The point is that your personality is shaped by your preferences and those preferences are still within you, even if they are sometimes covered up by the demands of life. It is the dynamic interaction of your set of preferences that produces what we call personality type.[19]

This exercise is designed to help you understand the meaning of the four preferences listed above. This is only an exercise, not a scientifically designed instrument. The exercise is divided into four sections: orientation, perception, decision making, and lifestyle.

Each number contains two questions that address opposite kinds of behaviors or traits. Using the scale underneath each set of descriptions, circle the number that best indicates your preferred ways of living. You may circle a number under each statement if you believe that both descriptions apply to you. The numbers on the scale below have these meanings:

5 - Always true for me
4 - True most of the time
3 - True about half the time
2 - Sometimes true
1 - Only occasionally true

Always go with your initial response. Try to think in terms of how you prefer to live, not how you think you should live. Try to express your own preference and not mirror what you think others expect of you. Here is a sample question.

Are you easily bored when you are alone?	Do you enjoy solitude in order to spend time in your own thoughts?
E-5 (4) 3 2 1 0	1 (2) 3 4 5-I

The scoring instructions are given at the end of the exercise. Read them *after* you have completed the exercise.

Orientation

1. Do you find that your attention flows naturally to the people and things around you?

   E-5   **4**   **3**   **2**   **1**   **0**

   Or, do you find that, whenever possible, you prefer to occupy yourself with your own inner world of thoughts and ideas?

   1   **2**   **3**   **4**   **5-I**

2. Would you characterize yourself as outgoing?

   E-5   **4**   **3**   **2**   **1**   **0**

   Or, would you describe yourself as basically a reserved person?

   1   **2**   **3**   **4**   **5-I**

3. Is your energy renewed by being with others?

   E-5   **4**   **3**   **2**   **1**   **0**

   Or, even though you enjoy others' presence, do you find that you need solitude to recharge your batteries?

   1   **2**   **3**   **4**   **5-I**

4. Are you rather easy to get to know?

   E-5   **4**   **3**   **2**   **1**   **0**

   Or, are you reluctant to allow others into your private world?

   1   **2**   **3**   **4**   **5-I**

5. Do you find it easy to think out loud?

   E-5   **4**   **3**   **2**   **1**   **0**

   Or, do you feel that you need to turn inward in order to collect and organize your thoughts before you speak?

   1   **2**   **3**   **4**   **5-I**

6. Are you rather expressive of your feelings?

   E-5   **4**   **3**   **2**   **1**   **0**

   Or, do you mostly keep your feelings to yourself?

   1   **2**   **3**   **4**   **5-I**

7. When you are under stress, do you seek the company of others in order to sort things out?

   E-5   **4**   **3**   **2**   **1**   **0**

   Or, when you are under stress, do you require a measure of seclusion so that you can pull things together?

   1   **2**   **3**   **4**   **5-I**

8. Do you tend to act first and think later?

   E-5   **4**   **3**   **2**   **1**   **0**

   Or, do you tend to reflect and reflect and (perhaps) eventually get around to action?

   1   **2**   **3**   **4**   **5-I**

Perception

1. Do you depend on your five senses in order to gather data about what's happening?

   S-5 **4** **3** **2** **1** **0**

   Or, do you rely more on your intuitions and hunches in order to form impressions about what's going on?

   1 **2** **3** **4** **5-N**

2. Do you prefer straightforward ways of speaking and writing—the more specific and concrete the better?

   S-5 **4** **3** **2** **1** **0**

   Or, do you like a speaker or writer to use images and symbols that allow you to engage your own imagination?

   1 **2** **3** **4** **5-N**

3. Are you an observer of tradition, one who does not easily break with custom?

   S-5 **4** **3** **2** **1** **0**

   Or, are you able to break with tradition whenever it seems restrictive and to lay aside customs that seem too cumbersome for a new situation?

   1 **2** **3** **4** **5-N**

4. Does the here and now keep your attention?

   S-5 **4** **3** **2** **1** **0**

   Or, are you fascinated by what could be and find that those possibilities occupy your thoughts?

   1 **2** **3** **4** **5-N**

5. Do you have trouble seeing the forest for the trees?

   S-5 **4** **3** **2** **1** **0**

   Or, are you a person who often cannot see the trees for the forest?

   1 **2** **3** **4** **5-N**

6. Are you a practical sort of person with a commonsense approach to things?

   S-5 **4** **3** **2** **1** **0**

   Or, are you an ingenious and inventive sort of person with a creative approach to things?

   1 **2** **3** **4** **5-N**

7. If someone hangs a new picture or puts a new plant on a table, will you almost always notice it?

   S-5 **4** **3** **2** **1** **0**

   Or, are you often rather unobservant of your surroundings?

   1 **2** **3** **4** **5-N**

8. Are you a steady, dependable kind of person who can be counted on for the long haul?

   S-5 **4** **3** **2** **1** **0**

   Or, do you tend to work by inspiration and find that when your vision for a task fades, so does your energy?

   1 **2** **3** **4** **5-N**

Decision making

1. Are you generally secure in basing your decisions on an objective analysis, weighing the pros and cons of a situation?

   Or, regardless of the pros-and-cons score are you more secure when you feel that your decision is being based on values that are important to you and others?

   T-5   **4**   **3**   **2**   **1**   **0**   **1**   **2**   **3**   **4**   **5-F**

2. Can you usually get on with your job, regardless of relational harmony?

   Or, do you find that harmonious relationships are essential for you to function effectively in a situation?

   T-5   **4**   **3**   **2**   **1**   **0**   **1**   **2**   **3**   **4**   **5-F**

3. Does making a critical evaluation come more naturally for you than speaking an appreciative word?

   Or, are you more spontaneous with an appreciative word than with a critical evaluation?

   T-5   **4**   **3**   **2**   **1**   **0**   **1**   **2**   **3**   **4**   **5-F**

4. When forced to choose, do you place truthfulness above tactfulness?

   Or, when you face a crunch, do you place tactfulness above truthfulness?

   T-5   **4**   **3**   **2**   **1**   **0**   **1**   **2**   **3**   **4**   **5-F**

5. Do you find that your contribution to a group often lies in your ability to help people see objectively?

   Or, do you find your contribution to others usually flows from your ability to empathize and to help people stay mindful of others' feelings?

   T-5   **4**   **3**   **2**   **1**   **0**   **1**   **2**   **3**   **4**   **5-F**

6. In conversation, are you more concise than expressive?

   Or, in conversations, are you more expressive than concise?

   T-5   **4**   **3**   **2**   **1**   **0**   **1**   **2**   **3**   **4**   **5-F**

7. Do you believe that people are more apt to make the wrong move if they go with their hearts rather than their heads?

   Or, do you believe that people are more likely to make the wrong move if they go with their heads rather than their hearts?

   T-5   **4**   **3**   **2**   **1**   **0**   **1**   **2**   **3**   **4**   **5-F**

8. Are you more impersonal, with more interest in things than in people?

   Or, are you more personal, with more interest in people than in things?

   T-5   **4**   **3**   **2**   **1**   **0**   **1**   **2**   **3**   **4**   **5-F**

Lifestyle

1. Do you prefer to plan your work and work with your plan?

   J-5   4   3   2   1   0

   Or, do you like to leave your schedule open so that you can respond to changing events?

   1   2   3   4   5-P

2. Do your basic contributions to a group often stem from being systematic, orderly, planned, and decisive?

   J-5   4   3   2   1   0

   Or, are the attributes which you bring to a group such things as spontaneity, open-mindedness, tolerance, and adaptability?

   1   2   3   4   5-P

3. Do you enjoy bringing things to completion—finishing the task?

   J-5   4   3   2   1   0

   Or, do you like the feeling of getting new things started and having many things going at the same time?

   1   2   3   4   5-P

4. Do you like to get the information you need and bring things to a decisive conclusion?

   J-5   4   3   2   1   0

   Or, is it hard for you to come to closure because you are unsure if you've gathered sufficient information?

   1   2   3   4   5-P

5. Are you the sort of person who likes having standard operating procedures and set routines for doing things?

   J-5   4   3   2   1   0

   Or, do you prefer trying out new and fresh ways of doing recurring tasks so that you won't get into a rut?

   1   2   3   4   5-P

6. Would the phrase "A place for every-thing and everything in its place" be descriptive of your lifestyle?

   J-5   4   3   2   1   0

   Or, are you more scattered and disorganized in your way?

   1   2   3   4   5-P

7. Is it unsettling for you to have matters up in the air and undecided?

   J-5   4   3   2   1   0

   Or, do you prefer keeping your options open for as long as possible, so you won't miss something?

   1   2   3   4   5-P

8. Is it a greater weakness for a person to be too laid-back than for a person to be too task-oriented?

   J-5   4   3   2   1   0

   Or, do you think that it may be a greater weakness when one is too task-oriented than for the one to be too laid-back?

   1   2   3   4   5-P

SCORING THE EXERCISE

1. Score each section of the exercise separately.
2. Add the numbers circled in each column.
3. Place your totals in the appropriate spaces below.

A. Orientation	E _____	I ____
B. Perception	S _____	N ____
C. Decision making	T _____	F ____
D. Lifestyle	J _____	P ____

4. Go back to the above and circle the letter in each set that has the highest score. The highlighted numbers suggest your type. The example below will guide you.

A. Orientation	E 15	I **30**
B. Perception	S 19	N **28**
C. Decision making	T **35**	F 20
D. Lifestyle	J 10	P **30**

In this example, the person's personality type may be INTP. The following chart interprets the personality traits highlighted in the above example.[20]

The following chart highlights the different types of personalities in relationship to their gifts or strengths, infirmities or weaknesses, nurture, or areas of development and growth needs.[21] In the first column we can associate the personality gifts to those four areas of thinking, feeling, sensing, and intuiting. The second column highlights weak spots or most vulnerable areas in relationship to the overall personality type. The nurture column provides areas where the differing personality types naturally nourish their spiritual lives. Finally, the growth needs area is an action step where each personality type could develop and mature. It is fascinating to understand how God has uniquely created us. As we mature spiritually, emotionally, and psychologically we will find that God does not confine us to a box. Life is a journey toward Christlikeness. Our responsibility is to allow Him to use us, warts and all.

HOW PERSONALITY TYPE INFLUENCES SPIRITUAL LIFE

	Creation gifts	Weak Spots	Nurture faith	Growth needs
ENERGIZERS **ESTP** **ESFP**	• action • altruism • adaptability • acceptance • artistry • appreciation	• allurement • seduction • brinkmanship • bravado • expediency • opportunism	• physical • spirituality of service • praying over experiences	• reflection • faithfulness
STABILIZERS **ISTJ** **ISFJ**	• thoroughness • persistence • practicality • prudence • methodicalness • dependability • common sense	• self-absorption • hiddenness • suspicion • prudishness • idolatry • perfectionism	• quietness • structured prayer • spiritual continuity	• self-assurance • playfulness • receptivity • spontaneity
CRUSADERS **ENFP** **ENTP**	• ingenuity • optimism • inspiration • creativity • originality • insight • perceptivity	• lack of focus • independence • inconsistency • unfaithfulness	• maintain stability • listening prayer • servanthood	• dependence on Christ • reflection
RENEWERS **INFJ** **INTJ**	• insight • vision • inspiration • motivation • possibility	• loneliness • restlessness • indulgence • overextended-ness	• imaging prayer • use of symbol • creative writing	• trust intuition • sharing insights • awareness • self-discipline • balanced life
ORGANIZERS **ESTJ** **ENTJ**	• leadership • structure • goal-direction • decisiveness • objectivity • formula	• tunnel vision • impersonality	• action & reflection • mental prayer • written prayer • stillness before God	• practice listening • seek feedback • reflection • flexibility • surrender of gifts
ANALYZERS **ISTP** **INTP**	• understanding • reasoning • commitment to justice • reservedness	• insensitivity • laziness • moodiness	• mental prayer • breath prayer • meditation	• feeling • giving leadership • empathy
ENCOURAGERS **ESFJ** **ENFJ**	• warmth • hospitality • loyalty • idealism • practicality • responsibility	• hypersensitivity • unreflectiveness • avoidance of unpleasantness	• community • compassion • affective prayer • personalizing • worship space	• realism • kindness to self • openness to critique
ENHANCERS **ISFP** **INFP**	• mission • purpose • warmth • quiet reserve • positivity • hopefulness • independence • flexibility • openness	• feelings of inadequacy • resistance to reason • reluctance to share • perfectionism	• personalizing • Scripture • spiritual journey • listening prayer	• Christ-conscious • receptivity to grace • cultivate relationships

The Myers-Briggs is only one of several personality profile tests. Others include DiSC, the Role Preference Inventory, and Taylor-Johnson Temperament Analysis. Our personalities influence the decision-making process in ways of which we are unaware unless we become students of ourselves.

As we proceed, each chapter will flow through the following outline:

- Case clarifications
- Decision-Making Tower
- Ethical guidelines
- Biblical issues
- Suggested approaches
- Conclusion
- Discussion questions

For us to make wise, ethical decisions, we need the Spirit of God bringing together the heart and the mind. We need others to challenge our thinking, asking tough questions that strengthen our confidence in this critical area of our ministry.

The ensuing cases contain real-life issues. Some of the stories will bring tears to your eyes while others will raise your blood pressure in anger. Our ultimate goal, however, is to use them as a means to an end: the making of wise, biblical decisions.

CHAPTER TWO

ABUSE INSIDE THE CHURCH

THE DEACON AND HIS DAUGHTER

THE FOLLOWING DILEMMA highlights one church's tension when scriptural principles are challenged by the loyalty a congregation has for one of its own members.

Steve and Jenny Leopold seemed to be a normal family. Their marriage had its difficult moments, but the members of First Church seemed to rally around them and, guided by the principles of Scripture, help them handle each crisis. The church looked to the Lord for His guidance, trusting that God's sovereignty would make sense to them. This always gave them hope in the midst of their growing pains.

One autumn evening something happened that changed the dynamic of First Church for a long time. Steve, a charter member and friend to many in the church, was arrested and indicted on first- and second-degree charges of child molestation. One year out of seminary, Pastor Harry was confronted with his greatest challenge in the ministry. The juvenile in question was Rebecca, Steve's stepdaughter. What complicated matters was the fact that Steve previously held a key leadership position in the church.

Pastor Harry became involved when Rebecca's boyfriend, David, called him. Rebecca had told him she might be pregnant by her stepfather. David was stunned and scared, and he decided Pastor Harry would be their safest ally. The pastor had developed a close friendship with one of the detectives in town. After hanging up the phone with David, Pastor Harry called Joe. Due to the nature of the situation and the state law, a juvenile officer was immediately called.

When Rebecca's parents received a telephone call from the juvenile officer, they too called Pastor Harry, asking him if he knew what kind of trouble Rebecca was in. He told them he would pick them up and they would go to the police station together. After the girl's stepfather was questioned, he made a statement indicting himself on several counts of child molestation.

The days following Steve Leopold's indictment were difficult for the families of First Church. Some could not even fathom the thought of incest. It was sickening, repulsive, unthinkable. Others called for the church to take immediate and strong action. Steve should have his membership removed and the people should treat him like a nonbeliever as Paul described in 1 Corinthians 5. Still, some challenged Pastor Harry to show Steve love and acceptance. Some of the Leopolds' closest friends met with Pastor Harry.

At a special meeting, Pastor Harry and the church leadership met with Steve to discuss the awkward situation. Unsure of exactly what to do since none of them had ever encountered this type of dilemma, the church board requested that Steve adhere to the discipline of "silent disclosure," to be observed for a period of one year. This meant Steve was to refrain from participating in the Lord's Supper, to give up any church involvement he had, and to be under the spiritual supervision and guidance of the church leadership. The matter was handled in a very compassionate and caring manner in order that restoration might occur. The issue of confidentiality and its relationship to biblical mandates was discussed.

Steve's response of denial and anger surprised Pastor Harry and the church leaders. He began accusing them of ruining his life and family. He felt the leadership of the church had no right to discipline him in this way and that they were acting unbiblically. For several months his actions displayed a rebellious and uncooperative spirit. Week after week he would sit with his family in the front pew, staring down Pastor Harry throughout the entire worship service. During the Sunday school hour Steve and his wife would disrupt Pastor Harry's teaching, accusing him of hypocrisy and immaturity. Steve's avoidance of responsibility and transference of his guilt blurred the real issue. As time dragged on, this began to cause other church members to question the action of the church leadership. Even though no public statement had been made from the pulpit or at any congregational meeting, word was getting around. In fact, some were waiting to see what First Church would do since the board's planned meeting concerning Steve was several weeks before his court date.

Eventually the newspapers got wind of the story, placing the church leadership in a compromising situation. First Church was located in a very small rural community that kept no secrets. A local billboard read, "You might not see much in our little town, but what you hear makes up for it." The small-town reporters repeatedly called Pastor Harry trying to get a lead article.

Pastor Harry kept silent during this period while being pressured by

Steve and Jenny's closest friends to forget about the church discipline for fear of what it would do to the church and the Leopolds' family. In effect, their loyalty to this couple was strong enough to overlook his actions and compromise the integrity of Scripture. The people were tired of being in the town's gossip column. Some of them just wanted to forget the events of the past six months.

Decision-Making Tower

When we place the principle components of this case through the four levels as outlined in the Decision-Making Tower, we discover the dilemma Pastor Harry and the church leadership faced regarding Steve Leopold's situation (see figure 2.1; review figures 1.2 and 1.3).

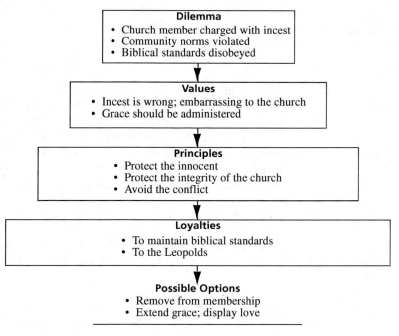

Dilemma
- Church member charged with incest
- Community norms violated
- Biblical standards disobeyed

Values
- Incest is wrong; embarrassing to the church
- Grace should be administered

Principles
- Protect the innocent
- Protect the integrity of the church
- Avoid the conflict

Loyalties
- To maintain biblical standards
- To the Leopolds

Possible Options
- Remove from membership
- Extend grace; display love

Figure 2.1

Ethical Guidelines

The Decision-Making Tower forces us to collect the data and research the legal parameters and biblical standards that need to be understood and followed. Like Pastor Harry, many of us don't formulate a plan until the phone rings. If we are to guide ourselves through this problem we need to become aware of our own feelings on the subject. Maybe you were a victim of abuse as a child. If that is the case then your personal baggage will rise to the surface. It is important that we maintain loyalty to biblical standards of church discipline, which, hopefully, lead to restoration. Although some will strongly try to persuade us to practice grace, in the end discipline will be the grace required.

With this in mind, the following personal guidelines will help us navigate through these rough waters.

- Be aware of your personal values.
- Don't lose your compassion for the victim.
- Gain confidence in your biblical understanding of love and justice.
- Strategize a plan of attack.

In the dilemma that confronted Pastor Harry, the emotions of some congregational members blurred their understanding of Scripture and the impact of Steve's actions on the church and on the community (not to mention on the family and on the child).

Biblical Issues

Although he was still new in the ministry, Pastor Harry was not alone. Early on he established a mentoring relationship with a seasoned pastor twenty-five miles away, with whom he met on a monthly basis. He called his mentor on the phone and sought his wisdom and counsel. After listening to the counsel of a "Barnabas," Pastor Harry also called his "Paul," a professor at the seminary he attended. These men gave him the confidence he needed and assured him that they would be praying for everyone involved in this difficult situation. They guided him through the biblical steps he needed to take with Steve. These men helped Pastor Harry begin the difficult process.

Pastor Harry unknowingly was modeling Timothy's relationship with Paul. He then refreshed himself with 1 Corinthians 5:1–5 and continued in prayer. Paul wrote,

> It is actually reported that there is sexual immorality among you, and of a kind that does not occur even among the pagans: A man has his father's wife. And you are proud! Shouldn't you rather have been filled with grief and have put out of your fellowship the man who did this? Even though I am not physically present, I am with you in spirit. And I have already passed judgment on the one who did this, just as if I were present. When you are assembled in the name of our Lord Jesus and I am with you in spirit, and the power of our Lord Jesus is present, hand this man over to Satan, so that the sinful nature may be destroyed and his spirit saved on the day of our Lord.

When Pastor Harry called a meeting to guide his church leaders he was better prepared yet still scared about the future of First Church. Is the biblical precedent to excommunicate the believer from the local fellowship without even considering other factors? Steve had been doing this ugly sin for the past three years. Just because he was caught, does that mean nothing should be done? After all, his crime was evident! Paul was adamant. In 1 Corinthians 5:4, he gave us the impression that the whole church should assemble and pass judgment on the man. In verse 5 he gave the Corinthian church even stronger words of admonition. He said, Hand him over to Satan. Put him out so he is severed from the fellowship. In so doing the Devil will punish him with physical affliction.

On the other hand, one of the First Church board members who had known Steve for a long time brought up Galatians 6:1: "Brothers, if someone is caught in a sin, you who are spiritual should restore him gently." To what extent does this passage apply to Steve's case? Isn't one sin as bad as another? Wasn't Christ's sacrifice on the cross meant to cover all sins small or large? Jesus portrayed a spirit of love and compassion. Isn't this the model we need to follow? The board member stressed the need for grace to be ministered to Steve. Only through grace would Steve and his family have the chance to work through this very difficult trial. After all, didn't God allow this to happen for some reason?

As the board discussed the situation and searched the Scriptures, they considered Paul's admonition to the believers in 2 Corinthians 2:5–11:

> If anyone has caused grief, he has not so much grieved me as he has grieved all of you, to some extent—not to put it too severely. The punishment inflicted on him by the majority is sufficient for him. Now instead, you ought to forgive and comfort him, so that he will not be overwhelmed by excessive sorrow. I urge you, therefore, to reaffirm your love for him. The reason I wrote you was to see if you would stand the test and be obedient in everything. If you forgive anyone, I also forgive him. And what I have forgiven—if there was anything to forgive—I have forgiven in the sight of Christ for your sake, in order that Satan might not outwit us. For we are not unaware of his schemes.

How do decision makers integrate this passage in 2 Corinthians, especially if somewhere in their pasts there has been sexual abuse? All the issues of the past come racing to the surface and can blur the ability to make sound decisions. The anger this issue provokes causes emotions to run high, because the thought of incest and the abuse of children is heart-tugging. We want justice, but the Word says we need to consider forgiveness. These were some of the biblical issues that Pastor Harry and his board had to sort through.

One anonymous scribe wrote, "To embark successfully on a career involving leadership demands courage. Once a person has decided the part he wishes to play in life, and is assured he is doing the work for which he is best endowed, and is satisfied that he is filling a vital need, then he needs the courage to tackle the problems he must solve."

Suggested Approaches

In the past, information regarding cases such as this one would have been less available. However, this author believes in the years to come many more such issues will challenge the doctrine and leadership of local churches. Which biblical example is right to follow? What are the appropriate steps a church should take? Are there any risks involved? This we know for sure:

> In all fifty states, the law requires clergy to divulge any infor-
> mation that involves child molestation. Two kinds of laws serve
> to limit, influence, or inform clergy privileged communications.
> First, child abuse reporting laws are in effect in all fifty states. . . .
> Second, as discussed in prior chapters, religious counselors have
> a duty to protect their counselees and to protect third parties who
> are in danger from the counselee.[1]

The outcome in churches of cases involving incest are greatly influenced by the tension between biblical precedence and relational loyalties.

A solution can be implemented from several perspectives. Following Mill's principle of utility, the church leadership should seek the greatest happiness for the greatest number of people. Therefore, they should spare the details, not mention the juvenile's name (even though it had appeared in the paper), and not risk the chance of a lawsuit.

While Mills' approach is unbiblical, too often it seems to be the one used. Many churches are reluctant to confront members concerning moral issues for fear of lawsuits resulting from administering church discipline. The pastor who desires a long tenure would much rather minister God's love and let the courts handle the offender. For other pastors, even though civil law requires reporting suspected abuse, the rationale for not informing the authorities seems to be, God's laws are higher than human laws. As a result, the embarrassment usually motivates the offender or family to move to another church where the problem continues until it is made public once again.

In cases such as incest, the greatest happiness might involve the greatest amount of emotional pain. Is the church willing to pay the price? If so, then Galatians 6:1 sets the precedent.

On the other hand, Kant's universal law has some validity. Yes, there is evil in our society. Does that mean we should push it under the rug because we are Christians? No! Should we tell the truth even though it might damage someone's reputation? Yes! In the final analysis, truth telling is much better than peacekeeping. If we hold to Kant's universal law, then Paul is absolutely right in 1 Corinthians 5.

According to Scripture the church represents the truth. Jesus said, "I am the way and the truth and the life" (John 14:6). The offender in question damages his own reputation by committing a heinous crime. The truth sets the precedent and the tone concerning the application of Scripture, but the situation was complicated even more because Steve and Jenny's marriage was crumbling. During the time, Jenny was engaged in an extramarital affair of her own. When the church began to disclose the truth about Steve and Jenny, the couple eventually lashed out in denial toward those who exposed their sin.

Finally, one needs to consider the Judeo-Christian ethic: "Love your neighbor as yourself." Unconsciously, this was the ethic that prevailed in the minds of many members of the church. Obviously it was very difficult to separate their feelings from Steve's actions, which created tension within the church. Taking this ethic a step further, some have mistakenly thought that as a loving, caring example of Christ's love the church body should overlook the situation entirely and hope no one talks about it. The church members should go on with their daily lives. Too often in many churches this is the approach taken.

Conclusion

The church leadership proceeded with the steps outlined in Scripture regarding church discipline and restoration. They understood Paul's words in 1 Corinthians but integrated them with the Matthew 18 passage of church discipline. The talk of the town seemed to be about the people at First Church. Though everyone knew the details, Pastor Harry refrained from discussing the situation for fear of a pending lawsuit by the Leopolds.

After a six-month period and incredible stress, anguish, and personal slander, the congregation voted to remove Steve's name from the church membership because of a rebellious spirit, failure to submit to church discipline, and "moral failure."

The meeting was held and the leadership chose not to mention the juvenile's name or share the details. The basis of their decision came after an extended period of prayer for this member and his stepdaughter.

The truth was essential so that discipline could be made effective. Reconciliation in the church is not truth that extends itself to gossip but truth as means of restoration.

In cases such as this, the victim often feels at fault in some way. With this in mind the church chose not to mention the stepdaughter's name, in order to protect her, to abide by the civil law, and to still carry out the necessary discipline according to Scripture. In doing this they were making the statement that she was not at fault but that her stepfather was responsible for his actions. In the final analysis the church became her support. One year went by before First Church started to return to normal.

Discussion Questions

- Discuss when 1 Corinthians 5 or Galatians 6:1 would apply to other similar situations.

- Examine Matthew 18 and develop a strategy for church discipline of someone like Steve.

- What steps does Scripture give for discipline as outlined in Matthew 18?

- Discuss with another pastor the steps you would follow if this were your church.

A CHURCH'S DYSFUNCTIONAL CYCLE

OFTEN THE CHRISTIAN community seeks to protect itself from the world to such an extreme that the church becomes a haven for dysfunctional and unbiblical behavior. The following case reflects a multifaceted example of ethical missteps that can happen in any church. Strong leadership and established ethical standards could have helped stop the cycle of abuse.

How had the "little secret" of one man's life come to dominate the lives of colleagues and parishioners? "O what a tangled web we weave, when first we practice to deceive!" (Sir Walter Scott).

Here is one example of a church's dysfunctional cycle of behavior.

My mouth was dry and cottony. Each syllable, one by one, had to be forced out. These were tough words to say to my pastor, boss, and ministry colleague, "Last April when I came across you and Linda arm in arm, I felt hurt that you betrayed your marriage and your ordination."

I had thought out my lines the day before, and they had been reviewed by the intervention counselor from the alcohol and drug abuse treatment facility. Now, speaking to Phil, I had begun with reassurance: "Phil, I am here because I care about you, I care about Carol and your children, and I care about our church." But still, I hesitated.

I had scrawled the word "eyes" across the top of my script because I wanted to be sure to maintain eye contact with Phil across the large conference table in the presbytery office. After all the suspicions and hurts of the past two years, I wanted this encounter to be clean.

"Two weeks ago on a Tuesday afternoon," I continued, "you came into the church office. Your speech was slurred, and I smelled alcohol on your breath. I felt angry that alcohol was back in your life. I'm asking you now to accept the help being offered today."

The search committee that first brought Phil to the church said from the beginning that they had found "a diamond in the rough." In his mid-thirties and just a few months older than I, Phil had served two previous churches for a total of ten years, the first as a solo pastor, the second with a couple of part-time support people.

Considering his record and potential, the committee thought it an acceptable risk to bring someone from a small church in a rural setting to a large church in a suburban setting.

Energetic and full of stories and humor, his sermons helped attract to our church young families and many previously disenchanted baby boomers. Clearly nonministerial, his pulpit manner attracted many who otherwise might have thought they didn't belong.

What the church did not know was that in addition to his giftedness, Phil would also bring his alcoholism, which had plagued him for a dozen of his thirty-six years. And at the same time he was interviewing with our search committee, he was involved in an adulterous relationship.

In fact, charges of inappropriate behavior with women had dogged him since his first pastorate. But presbytery officials thought Phil had put those problems behind him. And none of the people who were called as references had any concerns in this area.

For a year, none of us suspected anything wrong. We did know, however, that we were dealing with someone who showed flashes of energy, insight, and innovation but who had trouble carrying through on ideas, who seemed intimidated by the people he wanted to lead, and who wasn't always honest with those whose trust he needed to inspire.

When Phil failed to attend important meetings or make needed calls, I tried to tell myself those characteristics were part of the visionary personality. At the same time, I felt guilty that I was unable and increasingly unwilling to confront Phil and offer my help in overcoming those deficiencies.

I began to feel angry that people considered my gifts, especially in administration, the perfect match for Phil's. It seemed Phil's administrative laxness was simply shifting increasing administrative burdens to me.

After awhile, however, I got tired of these games. I supervised most of the full-time staff at Community Church. The first January Phil was with us, I brought a list of vacation requests, including my own, to Phil to take to the personnel committee for routine approval. After the meeting I asked Phil about the vacation requests and he assured me all was fine.

But the March report of the personnel committee meeting showed approval of only Phil's vacation dates. None of the other staff's dates were listed and Phil's vacation overlapped mine. When I asked Phil what had happened, he admitted he'd forgotten to bring the other dates in for review.

I don't like confrontations, and after Phil repeated several similar episodes with me and others, I quit raising issues.

Early on, Phil showed a tendency to strike up warm relationships with certain types of women—usually women between the ages of twenty-five and forty-five who were in good physical shape. Most were vivacious and outgoing but also displayed some sense of vulnerability—divorced women or young widows, those with emotionally unavailable husbands, or those enduring family or marital stress.

At first reports, the grapevine said that those women thought Phil just wanted a little understanding and reassurance: "He's really insecure, you know." Never the touchy-feely type, I concluded that my discomfort was due to my inhibitions.

One early autumn midafternoon at the beginning of his second year at the church, Phil came into the office after having been at home for several hours. He was staggering, his speech was slurred, and his breath was overpowering. He was talkative and much more friendly than normal. He was drunk.

For several months the secretaries had seen and smelled the signs of excessive drinking. Searching for a file in Phil's office, one secretary found an empty wine bottle. Another discovered a clearly "noncoffee odor" from Phil's ever-present coffee cup.

We had been offering an adult class on alcoholism, which one of the secretaries was taking. As the teacher had described alcoholic behavior—memory blackouts, inconsistent excuses, urgency about finances, preoccupation with health—the secretary found herself listening to Phil being described by someone who didn't even know him. But, unbelievable to me now, I still wasn't ready to accept the diagnosis.

Fall turned into winter, and the episodes continued. Often I had smelled nothing when the secretaries told me they thought Phil had been drinking. I'd ask if it might have been mouthwash or cough drops.

Nonetheless, on two more occasions I recognized clearly that Phil was influenced by alcohol. I shared my growing concern with a good friend who was also a part-time pastor on staff. He responded that he had seen Phil under the influence one Sunday morning before the early service. It was becoming harder and harder to deny the problem.

Not knowing what else to do, I decided to talk to an elder on our personnel committee.

"Tom, I have some concerns about Phil," I began. "I think it's more than his work style and habits that others have mentioned. What I say must be kept in strict confidence. I am making no charges, and if what I say makes no sense to you, you're free to forget this conversation ever took place."

Tom was a personnel professional. On the one hand he probably couldn't be shocked easily, but he was also a pastor's son and a pastor's father and held the ministry in high esteem. I was having a hard time reading the expression on his face.

"I have reasons to believe," I continued, "that Phil may be having a problem with drinking, with seeing other women, and with honesty."

Two months after my conversation with Tom, I had my second conference with a personnel committee elder. John was a backpacking buddy and an old friend. He was a pro at troubleshooting staff problems. John was newly elected to the Session and had been chair of the pastor nominating committee that had selected Phil. His first personnel committee meeting had been a shocker. As a result of my and others' comments, they had met without Phil to discuss the rumored drinking problem.

Summer had come and with it the vacation season. Before we could leave for a week of camping, though, I received one and then another phone call: Had I heard about Phil's sermon on Sunday?

In the course of discussing Galatians 5:1 and freedom from spiritual slavery, Phil surprised the congregation with bad news and then reassured them with good news. "Several years ago," he said, "when I first came to this community, I was under a lot of pressure to succeed, and I began to drink too much. But when I realized I had become a slave to alcohol, I quit drinking. Now I know that to say yes to the freedom promised in Christ is to say no to alcohol."

Apparently it played out well. The congregation was impressed with the candor and honesty. They respected the willingness to be vulnerable and they rejoiced in the victory.

I, on the other hand, was furious. Didn't they realize they had been conned? "Several years ago, when I first came to this community"—

several years? It had been less than two years! Certainly someone should have caught that. And my calendar, where I had started noting Phil's erratic behavior, showed but five weeks since I'd seen Phil in the office drunk.

I felt betrayed. After my agony of the previous two years, he just gets up and gets better! The bitterness that had been directed at Phil turned inward. I was ashamed of my attitude and actions of the past year.

After Phil's return from vacation, my wife had asked me to seek professional help if for nothing else than to find a way to manage my own stress. I grew up in a family where little disagreements were ignored and big disagreements ended in anger and hurt. I learned early on to avoid disagreement at all cost. However, the cost was paid inside me.

At the church, for instance, rather than confront the situation, I was rescuing the congregation from Phil by denying and hiding the consequences of his actions. Furthermore, I had hoped someone or something would rescue me in the same way. When the elders were reluctant to take firm action, I felt betrayed and angry.

When I finally recognized such patterns, I was able for the first time in a year to make firm statements and take uncompromising stands. The new-found strength of my convictions came at the same time that a small number of key elders and members had begun to look at Phil with new eyes. The confession sermon, which had played well with most, had not settled easily with some.

Phil's last episode with drinking at the church came on a Tuesday afternoon in late September. He had been out of the office, ostensibly on a pastoral call, and returned to the office intoxicated. This time, rather than pretending "maybe it's only mouthwash," I picked up the phone and called a nearby and well-informed elder and said, "Phil has just come by the church. He's drunk. I thought you should know, because you're in a position to do something about it."

The next several days were a flurry of phone calls. Though the confusion and anxiety had hardly disappeared, important changes had taken place. Even the presbytery was growing concerned. The reality of the problem and responsibility for it was being borne by those given authority in our system—elders and presbytery officials, not subordinate church staff. Denial had been replaced, at least partially, by a plan for remedial action. Phil would be asked to admit himself to an alcohol-treatment program. In love and concern, the church would pay all noninsured expenses and full continuing salary.

A month later, and in the interest of his own recovery, Phil asked to be relieved of his responsibilities at First Church.[2]

Decision-Making Tower

When we consider our dilemma through the eyes of the associate pastor, here is what the Decision-Making Tower looks like (see fig. 2.2).

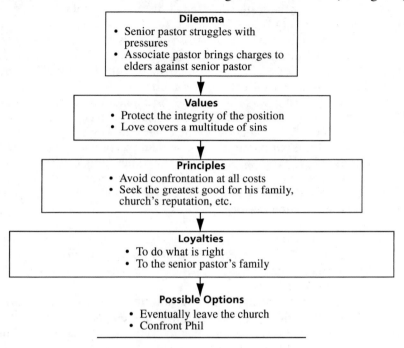

Dilemma
- Senior pastor struggles with pressures
- Associate pastor brings charges to elders against senior pastor

Values
- Protect the integrity of the position
- Love covers a multitude of sins

Principles
- Avoid confrontation at all costs
- Seek the greatest good for his family, church's reputation, etc.

Loyalties
- To do what is right
- To the senior pastor's family

Possible Options
- Eventually leave the church
- Confront Phil

Figure 2.2

Ethical Guidelines

This case involves a series of ethical choices made by multiple parties. It reveals the pain of many lives that culminated from misplaced adherence to confidentiality because of personality weaknesses and from the abuse of the office of the senior pastor. The reality manifests the circumstances under which many decisions are made. The cycle of moral failure became apparent when Phil's problem was finally highlighted in a broader context.

Consider the ethical choices made by the following individuals and organizations.

Phil chose to lie because of the early patterns set in his life. His lying became so habitual that it became the norm. His lying was also used to justify his behavior and to serve as a means of protection for his wife and family. When finally confronted, Phil still denied his behavior by rationalizing his personality. Accompanying Phil's denial was also the acting out or transference of behavior that was manifested in his inability to make wise choices.

The associate pastor also chose to avoid the problems because of personal insecurities that were fed by the fact that he too failed to recognize his personality strengths and weaknesses. Eventually the precedent of telling the truth superseded his personal agenda and gave him the strength to confront.

Some ministers, however, suffer from underassertiveness. Their egos are so small that humility becomes a vice. These people have difficulty leading a congregation and confronting persons with either the demands of the Gospel or the specifications for a job.[3]

The associate pastor was stuck in the third quadrant of the Decision-Making Tower, seeing the situation as a crisis between confrontation and personality issues. Without considering other philosophies or strategies in the decision-making process, the associate pastor categorized Phil's behavior of lying, womanizing, and substance abuse through one particular framework. Even a Judeo-Christian love ethic would have recognized the red flags in regard to Phil's behavior. Here are some personal guidelines to consider:

- Know your own personality type and how you interact with others.
- Let Scripture guide you in this type of confrontation.
- Proclaim the truth.

The congregation had lived out the familiar proverb, "See no evil, speak no evil, hear no evil." For them, lying was justified in terms of some higher value: the appearance that everything was all right and the church was a safe place. For the congregation, truth telling was a principle in Scripture to be read and discussed but seldom practiced in the church.

The denomination clearly practiced what might be cited as the Judeo-Christian love ethic, but its manifestation in the form of denial rooted in love was damaging a pastor, several families, and a church.

Biblical Guidelines

This biblical issue is similar to the time when Paul confronted Peter in Galatia for being two-faced with the Jews and Gentiles. Although Peter was not drunk like Phil, he brought others down because of his position in the church.

Paul writes in Galatians 2:11–13:

> When Peter came to Antioch, I opposed him to his face, because he was clearly in the wrong. Before certain men came from James, he used to eat with the Gentiles. But when they arrived, he began to draw back and separate himself from the Gentiles

because he was afraid of those who belonged to the circumcision group. The other Jews joined him in his hypocrisy, so that by their hypocrisy even Barnabas was led astray.

Even Barnabas! When I think of Barnabas, words like *mature, balanced, encouraging, giving,* and *focused* all come to my mind. Since Pentecost, Peter was a changed man. Though he was unschooled, quick to open his mouth, and at times lacked long-term memory, the Holy Spirit had given him a spirit of liberty and the ability to articulate the Gospel with clarity and power. As a result many had come to Christ and the church was growing phenomenally. Peter even turned the heads of the Pharisees. His apparent hypocrisy was so misleading because of who he was and how God was using him that even Barnabas was carried away in sin.

Paul could have forgotten the whole matter. Just think of the influence Peter was having among the nonbelievers. God was using him. So what is one little incident? Let's just overlook this in light of all his other accomplishments.

Phil's situation was no different. For almost two years his associate denied and rationalized Phil's substance abuse and failure to meet up to biblical standards as a pastor. The associate too was carried away. By neglecting his personal character development he was lowering the standard of his calling. After all, Phil was dynamic, a good teacher, the elders believed in him, and he was attracting new people to the church. I wonder how many Phils there are in ministry today? What we look at all too often are numbers, visibility, and presentation. Instead, characteristics like integrity, personal growth, or accountability should be highlighted.

In a day when radio preachers flood the airwaves and publishing houses churn out books by the hundreds, pastors are pressured to preach like Charles Swindoll and write like Max Lucado. External pressures, the church's bottom line, rapid growth rates, and strong leadership stretch us like rubber bands. In the course of stretching, some of us break. We leave the ministry disillusioned, get caught up in vices, or neglect our families. We tend to defend our own while at the same time jealously attacking their weaknesses. Solomon was right when he wrote Proverbs 4:23: "Above all else, guard your heart, for it is the wellspring of life." In any case, this is one reason why Phil's associate pastor had such a difficult time with his position and Phil's behavior.

There are times when we need to look to Scripture and tear ourselves away from the mirages we want to see. The words of Paul to Timothy apply to Phil. First Timothy 3:1–3, "Here is a trustworthy saying: If anyone sets his heart on being an overseer, he desires a noble task. Now the overseer must be above reproach, the husband of but one wife, temperate, self-controlled, respectable, hospitable, able to teach, not given to drunkenness, not violent but gentle, not quarrelsome, not a lover of money." By denying the accusations made against Phil, the elders were ignoring Paul's words to Timothy.

Before considering suggested approaches, let us look at the different factors that enabled the situation to linger. In each of these factors direct confrontation needed to be administered. Although this may seem harsh, the failure to do so was the reason for this church's dysfunctional cycle.

Phil. The drinking, the womanizing, the dishonesty, and the spiritual emptiness were responses, coping mechanisms, learned by Phil early in life as he reacted to pressures and problem relationships.

The fact that neither Phil nor his references mentioned any alcohol or infidelity problems during the search and interview process was not an act of deliberate deception. The insidious element of the problem was denial—from Phil's perspective, it seemed to be "another Phil" who stopped for a drink on the way to a hospital call and who sometimes forgot to make the call.

Associate Pastor. His readiness to avoid conflict and deny problems, his rescuing Phil by holding the church together when Phil neglected his duties, his delight in the affirmation he received for holding the church together, and his willingness to ignore the needs of his family for the "higher calling" of ministry were behaviors he, too, had learned at an early age.

Leadership. Each staff member and each elder also brought into their circle bits and pieces from his or her distinct background. Tom, having been raised in a ministry family, too easily sympathized with Pastor Phil. John, the executive problem solver, saw the situation as a professional difficulty that management techniques could solve.

Congregation. Over its sixty-five-year history, First Church developed its own personality and learned to respond in its own way to such difficulties. Extramarital affairs on the part of two previous pastors and a divorce in the life of another have made First Church members reluctant to know about the personal lives of their ministers; the church leaders were afraid of what they might find and might be forced to do. In the face of overwhelming evidence of something wrong, they wanted to believe that nothing was.

Denomination. The congregation was never told that there were issues other than alcoholism that affected Phil's ability to return to ministry. Even when evidence of at least one extramarital affair emerged, the presbytery made it clear that there would be no discussion of church discipline in this case.

Suggested Approaches

The associate pastor described his personality type as one that shied away from any form of confrontation. As a result, this not only prolonged the situation but created a great deal of stress in his life and in his family. If he had understood his personality type earlier, he may have been able to find someone in a position to confront Phil with the truth about his life and vices.

One approach for the associate pastor would have been to go outside the church to the presbytery or some other denominational authority. This may be a district superintendent or a seminary or Bible school professor. They could meet in a neutral environment where the pressures inside the church wouldn't be as great. His fears would have been lessened and he could have released some of his own tensions.

The responsibility for making ethical decisions is not intended to rest on one person's shoulders. When Christian love begins to move away from its biblical moorings it takes on the form of deception.

As the associate thought back to that ministry, he summed up his experience with these words: "Throughout those two troubled years, I was plagued with guilt over my disloyalty. I denied the existence of problems because I did not want to selfishly undermine Phil's ministry or the church's life."[4]

Conclusion

The case of Phil gives us a chance to look inside a multiple-staff church and consider the dynamics that create tension and growth. From my experience as a solo pastor and as a staff member of a large multiple-staff church, I am convinced of the need to develop a team approach to ministry. Understand that your spiritual giftedness, personality styles, theological moorings, and philosophies of ministry all blend together for what might be a long or short tenure. The constant tension between honesty and criticism is cause for personal reflection. What is important to one staff member might not be to another. But that is how God gifted us and wired us. This is the uniqueness of the body of Christ.

For the many who pastor solo, I would encourage you to meet regularly with other pastors for prayer and encouragement. Create fellowship where you discuss theological issues and personal styles. Get your families involved with each other. Spouses need to know they are not alone in their unique role.

One final word: if you find yourself out of control in some area of your life—your temper, envy, finances, marriage, children, whatever—don't be too proud to seek help.

Discussion Questions

- Who should the pastor be accountable to and to what extent?

- Work through 1 Timothy 3, the characteristics of an overseer, and discuss these with your elders or church leadership.

- How does envy and jealousy show up in your ministry?

- How do you work through it?

CHAPTER THREE

AIDS AMONG THE FLOCK

SHATTERED INNOCENCE

THE FOLLOWING ARTICLES appeared in the *Chicago Tribune* and the *Chicago Sun-Times* in response to an AIDS policy drafted by the Christian Education committee of the Moody Memorial Church in Chicago in the spring of 1990. The issue of the spread of HIV and how it should be handled is being addressed by more and more churches. Since this incident, much more research has surfaced. Still, churches need to understand how they might respond when an HIV-infected person comes walking through the front doors.

"Bible school bars boy, 5, with AIDS"

For Walt and Terry Rucker, it is a matter of faith.

Their fundamental Christian beliefs drew them to the Moody Church on the near North Side. The same beliefs drew them to a five-year-old AIDS-infected child they have taken into their home in the Ravenswood neighborhood.

But now the church has banned the boy from its Sunday school classes.

The Ruckers, foster parents of the boy, have been told by the Moody Church to stop bringing the child to the Bible school there because of fears he could spread the disease to other children.

News of the ban came just a week after Ryan White, an Indiana teenager who was initially barred from his school because he had AIDS, was eulogized for his personal strength in helping the nation toward overcoming fears that the virus could be transferred through casual contact.

Walt, a slender, bearded man who turned forty-six on Thursday, said he and his wife, who have attended the church since 1980, were surprised by the ban.

"We thought with Ryan White, all that had been settled," Walt Rucker said.

Rev. Erwin Lutzer, pastor of the Moody Church, 1609 N. LaSalle Street, issued a statement Thursday, saying "the matter is under review."

"The boy was asked to refrain from coming to Sunday school to give us time to think it through," Lutzer's statement said. "No final decision has been made."

A church staff person said the couple and the boy "are not barred from coming to church services, but we asked if the child not join the preschool Sunday school class."

The staffer said the decision was made out of concern that there were unanswerable questions about how the AIDS infection is spread, such as "children putting toys in their mouths."

The boy, whose name the couple want to keep confidential to protect him, was born with the virus. Two months ago, the Department of Children and Family Services took the boy from his AIDS-infected mother out of concern that she was no longer able to care for him.

Walt, a psychologist, and Terry, a nurse who has worked in a hospital AIDS ward in Chicago, took the boy into their home.

The boy is the second person with AIDS the couple has assisted. The other person, a thirty-eight-year-old woman named Amelia, died in 1988.

"We weren't afraid to have Amelia live with us. I was not afraid to have my wife work with AIDS patients," Rucker said.

Though the boy has lived with them for only about two months, Rucker refers to him as "my son" and the boy calls him "Daddy."

Their voices mixed easily as the boy laughed and got ready for bed Thursday night with his foster father's help.

Walt Rucker said a church with an antiabortion stance that encourages all women to give birth, even those who would pass AIDS on to their babies, should not then turn away infected children.

"We strongly support the church's position on pro-life," he said. "We do not support the church's position on not taking a child with AIDS."

He thought the fears about the boy posing a health risk were irrational. "We think fears about that from some church members are groundless."[1]

"Moody reverses ban; AIDS boy to return to classes"

A five-year-old boy banned from Sunday school because he has AIDS can return to classes, officials of the Moody Church said Friday in a reversal of their original decision.

Church officials made the announcement at a hastily called news conference following publicity about the decision to ban the child known as "Joey."

Walt and Terry Rucker, foster parents of the boy and longtime members of the North Side nondenominational evangelical church, said in a statement they were pleased by the decision.

"There are many more children that either have AIDS or are HIV positive . . . and there is a need for more foster families," they said.

The church's pastor, Erwin Lutzer, said, "What we have decided to do is shift the burden of responsibility from us as a church to parents. As of now, we will welcome children who have AIDS into our Sunday school. We will simply let parents know. They have the freedom to keep their children from attending Sunday school."

Asked if public outcry played a part in the church's reversal, Lutzer said, "To a certain extent, yes."

Even as Lutzer made the announcement, members of the AIDS Coalition to Unleash Power, or ACT-UP, protested outside the church, banging on the locked doors as they chanted, "Remember Ryan White"—the Indiana boy who recently lost his five-and-a-half-year struggle with the deadly acquired immune deficiency syndrome.

The Ruckers said they have received "positive and overwhelming" support, but are concerned that the attention may threaten Joey's anonymity.

"Our intention was not to embarrass the church," they said.

"We welcome the opportunity to take our foster child to Moody. We hope that the final outcome of this attention will be to place all of the children that are still awaiting homes."[2]

[One final note: "Joey," the little boy, died in 1995 due to complications caused by the AIDS virus. He was ten years old.]

Decision-Making Tower

The issue of AIDS is a highly explosive topic in our society. The message of the church has ranged from, "They got what they deserve," to "They are God's children; we need to love them even more." Differing values, a high degree of compassion, and greater understanding of the disease all converge to create a potpourri of opinions. Rural or urban, the church is now having to come to terms with how it embraces and handles adults or children with the HIV virus. The case at Moody Church in 1990 opened a can of worms in the church community. Here is a simple analysis of the case (see fig. 3.1).

Ethical Guidelines

As AIDS-related cases impact the church on a more frequent basis, there will be increasing tension between strict adherence to a church's policy and biblical modeling of Christ's love to those with HIV. When Jesus was asked which was the greatest commandment, he replied, "You shall love the Lord your God," and second, "You shall love your neighbor as yourself." The church as the body of Christ is admonished to practice the "one another" passages of Scripture; encourage one another, love

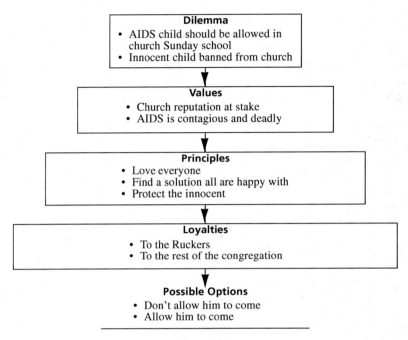

Figure 3.1

one another, bear one another's burdens, be patient with one another, teach one another, and so on. In this particular case, the Ruckers' passion for AIDS children multiplied the love factor in Scripture and the principles for how they lived. Moody Church, on the other hand, was unaware of how this sensitive issue would impact the rest of the body, especially considering the recent death of Ryan White and all the publicity surrounding his school's decision to prevent him from attending classes.

Since the Moody Church incident, there has been a tremendous amount of awareness and education relating to the HIV virus. With more and more celebrities forcing the issue for awareness and education, today's churchgoers are more in the know. The church needs to consider the following:

- Develop an infectious disease policy (refer to the appendix at the back of the book to guide your thinking) before you are confronted with such a situation.
- Preach a biblically related sermon series or initiate teaching dealing with difficult social issues, including the HIV virus, and their impact on the church.

- Understand how the truth needs to be communicated to the congregation.

These ethical guidelines will help prevent your congregation from boiling over on this sensitive topic and keep it from simmering as they address the various factors involved.

Biblical Issues

For some this might simply be a case where the obvious principle is to practice unconditional love. The Lord used the prophet Hosea and his relationship to Gomer to show how great a love He has for his people.

> When the LORD began to speak through Hosea, the LORD said to him, "Go, take to yourself an adulterous wife and children of unfaithfulness, because the land is guilty of the vilest adultery in departing from the Lord." So he married Gomer daughter of Diblaim, and she conceived and bore him a son. (Hos. 1:2–3)

Hosea obeyed God, and Gomer bore three children. Hosea loved her in spite of her rebellion and unfaithfulness, clearly portraying for us God's model of loving the unlovable. You might be saying, "Hosea is different from an AIDS child continuing in a church Sunday school." In practicality yes, but in principle no. God wanted to show to the nation of Israel His unconditional love and forgiving heart. The Ruckers felt compelled to show compassion and favor to AIDS children, who need Christ in a personal way and would experience His love through them.

It's like the story of the little girl who was frightened during a thunderstorm. When her dad went in to comfort her, he prayed and reassured her that Jesus was always with them. Her reply, "Daddy, I know, but I want Jesus with skin on!" As the body of Christ, isn't it our responsibility to show compassion, to walk our talk?

After all, even Jesus, in Mark 6:34, was moved by what He saw as He and His disciples landed on the shore. "When Jesus landed and saw a large crowd, he had compassion on them, because they were like sheep without a shepherd." Scripture says He taught them, fed them, healed them, and manifested love. His compassion went beyond words. This is what drew so many to Him, some for selfish reasons but many because He was a picture of hope and peace. The words of Scripture move people in different ways. Some are called to prayer, others to action. This is the uniqueness of the body of Christ.

But didn't Jesus say in the Sermon on the Mount, "Let your 'Yes' be 'Yes,' and your 'No,' 'No'" (Matt. 5:37)? He was speaking to those who were using oaths to confirm the truth because their word was in question.

If we have developed and implemented a policy, we need to adhere to its guidelines. For those who don't like the waters to be muddied, making an issue black and white is very important. This may be a result of their personalities or an inability to feel the pain of others.

Our comfort zones are stretched to new limits. As parents we become like a mother bear protecting her cubs. Even in Jesus' day, He was questioned for spending time with tax collectors, sinners, and publicans. What will be said of us? The issue between compassion and protection will inevitably be the balance we must find.

Suggested Approaches

It could be argued that the best approach is to tell the truth and deal with the consequences. Consider the treatment of tuberculosis fifty years ago or the medical laws that restricted infected students from returning to school without a medical release. This approach, although not very people-sensitive, will eliminate any policy problems for those who are driven by formulas. The truth-telling approach will either encourage anyone to come to Sunday school or will restrict all children who do not meet certain conditions. This is usually seen in blanket infectious disease policies formulated by many churches. How these policies are enforced is another issue.

If we consider implementing this approach we must also ask ourselves the following question. Is it ethically permissible to disclose that a child in a large Sunday school nursery has AIDS? From a Kantian perspective, definitely yes, especially since most children share toys, suck on the same items, and have diapers that need changing. In order for this truth-telling approach to be effective, a local church must prepare the congregation for the potential of such a case. Preparation will help establish the policy as considerate and reasonable.

On the other hand, the Judeo-Christian love ethic is another approach when considering AIDS cases. This approach will continue to be a source of tension for many churches especially when children are involved. The popular book *In His Steps* asks the question, "what would Jesus do?" Would He write a policy or simply love them? And to what degree? Those who have trouble with AIDS-infected people may hold to a misguided Judeo-Christian ethic similar to Pharisaism, which arbitrarily selects applications of love or virtue and judges life according to them. This would be the defense applied to neutralize those with overzealous compassion.

In order for a Judeo-Christian love ethic to apply, good communication with the parents must be a priority. Talking the walk and walking the talk will go miles with parents who feel called to invest their lives and love in AIDS-infected children.

Finally, for many, love in the Rucker case is displayed by an integration of Mill's "greatest happiness" principle. Were the Ruckers treated fairly and in turn was the church treated fairly regarding confidentiality? The Ruckers modeled Christlike love by adopting AIDS children. While trying to work out, as Mill's law states, the greatest good for all parties involved, the church needed to buy time and play catch-up. Unfortunately, the media had recently spotlighted AIDS children and the Ruckers' dilemma soon placed Moody Church in the media spotlight. On the heels of the death of Ryan White, the media salivated like dogs waiting for another bone to chew on. Their bone happened to be Moody Church. So much attention was given to this story that it even landed in newspapers across the ocean. What began as a church playing catch-up quickly turned into a case of first-amendment privileges.

AIDS cases need to be worked through Mill's framework because as more and more people contract the virus, their status and age will increasingly vary. Recent studies have indicated that every hour in America a teenager is infected with the AIDS virus. Would a teenager be given the same edict? Upon initial reaction it is understandable to prefer a truth-telling ethic, especially since the medical community seems to waffle or, as some have assumed, has withheld key information on the spread of the virus.

Most cases will not be in the spotlight like the Moody Church case, but every one will demand the same energy and prayer. In the final analysis the church will be forced to strike a balance between love and human nature.

Conclusion

In the final analysis it is important for pastors to discuss the Rucker case with the leadership of the church. Ask the question made popular by Hewlett Packard: "What if?" Discuss hypothetical cases. In so doing you will all be on the same page when the situation comes to your church. The sensitive issue of AIDS and children stirs up emotions that sometimes tend to overlook even biblical guidelines. The church is simultaneously called on to be a pillar of truth and justice coupled with an emergency care clinic to heal, love, and encourage those in need. Prepare yourself and your people ahead of time if at all possible. In the end, all will grow, and the love of Christ will be understood in a new light.

Discussion Questions

- Discuss with your church leadership how your church would go about handling such a crisis.

- Are you aware of AIDS support groups in your area? If so, invite them to give their insight on how you can better minister to families who care for AIDS children.

- Brainstorm and create a questionnaire asking your congregation how they would feel if an AIDS child started coming to your Sunday school.

THE FOUR-LETTER WORD THAT HAUNTS PASTORS

THE FOLLOWING CASE ILLUSTRATES how one pastor faced the issue of HIV/ AIDS with love and discernment while counseling a married couple. His wisdom was instrumental not only in ministering Christlike love to the husband who had AIDS but also in getting his church family involved as ministers of the body of Christ.

Sue and Jim began dating as juniors in high school, and their romance continued as they entered the same college. Dorm life was very progressive, and during their sophomore year they were able to room together for the remaining three years. After graduation they decided to marry because Sue was expecting. They wanted a church wedding, even though they had never been religious, and were married by a local pastor.

Six months after the wedding, a lovely daughter named Rachel was born to them, and the stresses of life seem to multiply unexpectedly. Jim was now working longer hours to provide an adequate income. The extra money, however, didn't seem to satisfy his need to find fulfillment. With greater work responsibility came more time away from home. Jim was given an assignment on the West Coast to begin his firm's California division. Every Sunday evening he would fly west and return home late Friday night.

As the days and weeks went by, his commitment to Sue was tested more and more. His emotions seemed out of control. While spending a late evening with Mary, a coworker, he fell into temptation, crossed the line, and committed adultery.

Jim's guilt made him miserable, but he hid his guilt from Sue. Something had changed, however; he was losing his passion for her. With each week his intimacy with his coworker continued to replace his feelings for his wife. Sue began to sense something was wrong and confronted him. Jim told her the truth and with little resistance from either of them, they decided it would be in their best interests to divorce.

Jim lived in California with Mary for two years until tragedy struck. While on their way to dinner one evening, they were in a serious car accident. Mary died at the scene, and he was in serious condition. After his recovery, Mary's death haunted him. His inability to grieve and process the loss were overwhelming. He began sleeping with prostitutes to rid himself of the pain.

Remarkably, Jim kept climbing the corporate ladder, all the time avoiding his feelings and covering up his illicit activities. He received a promotion that involved less travel and moved back to his hometown. During a meeting, Jim was introduced to Randy, a new client who was a Christian. Jim had to spend time working with Randy and began to see and hear of the changed life a person can have because of Jesus Christ. After several months, Jim trusted Christ as his Savior and turned his life around. He felt compelled to contact Sue. Unknown to him, Sue had received Christ the year before and was already praying for Jim. They began to see each other and talked about remarriage.

But something else had changed. Jim was unable to shake a bad cough and was sick more often. At the urging of Randy, Jim went to a doctor and found out he had acquired the HIV virus. Jim found support and confidentiality in his friend Randy and then decided to tell Sue the news. He also confessed his past promiscuity. After several weeks of prayer and reflection, she realized she still loved him. They remarried and began attending Cornerstone Church.

Shortly after they began attending, they met with the pastor. Here is how he described the events that followed.

"Jim was open with me about his previous life and illness, and I committed to complete confidentiality. Both Jim and Sue seemed to handle the reality of Jim's illness with a great deal of strength and faith, and they quickly made a place for themselves at the church. This was interesting to watch because they were different from the kind of folks who usually joined our church. And they loved church life. Their need for emotional and spiritual support was met through the church community.

"One afternoon Jim stopped in my office and asked me if he could share his testimony with the congregation. I was optimistic about the overall response of our congregation, but there was a real risk that Jim and Sue would be alienated from some of the people they loved and from whom they needed continued support. There was also the fear that Jim would lose his job if word got around about his illness. He needed his income and benefits to support his family and pay for medical treatment.

"We agreed that since Jim was still well enough to work, confidentiality was a must. As one pastor said, this decision could be called 'survival ethics.' I believe in honesty and openness. However, the demands of the situation—Jim's need for income—meant that Jim should not share his testimony with the congregation just yet. When Jim could no longer work, confidentiality would no longer be an issue. It would also be at that point, we all agreed, that he share his testimony and look to the congregation for support.

"As Jim's health deteriorated, we decided to contact four couples and ask them to especially support Jim and Sue. I called them and asked them to come to my office after the service one Sunday morning, and I gently disclosed the situation.

"First, I suggested, they needed to go home and talk with their families before committing themselves to this special ministry.

"Second, I stressed how important confidentiality was at that point. It was of paramount importance that no one else in the church besides them and their families knew all the facts. I also explained to them that I would be teaching an evening series called How Jesus Loves His Sheep.

"We also discussed how to handle the Sunday morning service when Jim would share his testimony and reveal his illness to the congregation.

"Soon the Sunday morning came when Jim shared his life and pain. There wasn't a dry eye in the congregation. They rallied around him like champions, checking up on Sue and Rachel as well as doing all they could to make him feel comfortable. After several bouts of *pneumocytis carinii* pneumonia, Jim died just three months after sharing his testimony."

Decision-Making Tower

Consider how one pastor unknowingly worked methodically through the Decision-Making Tower and framework at different times adjusting his strategy as the issue of confidentiality changed. In this case the pastor was deeply concerned about how to balance the reality of AIDS hysteria and the confidentiality necessary to protect Jim's job with this couple's need for emotional and spiritual support from the church community.

Ethical Guidelines

The dilemmas this pastor wrestled with were practical issues that impacted the couple financially and spiritually. If the facts were given all at once, consider the outcome: possible loss of job, loss of insurance, and added financial stress that might hinder the support given by the church community.

Not having previously dealt with the issue of AIDS, the pastor knew his congregation well enough to say, "I was optimistic about the overall response of our congregation." In light of the situation with Jim and Sue, the following personal guidelines need to be understood.

- Make sure you are a shepherd to your congregation—know them well.
- Giving the facts all at once is not always the best medicine.
- People will react differently no matter how well you give the facts.

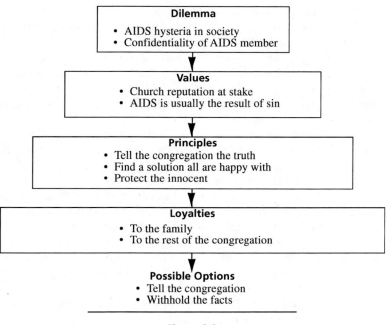

Figure 3.2

It is important for pastors to communicate openly with adults infected with the HIV virus. Regardless of how they contracted the virus, their presence will impact a whole congregation. These guidelines are given in order for you to walk through this mine field with as few casualties as possible.

Biblical Issues

The stigma of AIDS causes some to judge, become angry, and even uncaring. Many immediately ask the question, How did the person get it? In light of all the publicity regarding HIV/AIDS, our prejudices against those infected by the HIV virus has manifested itself in legalistic attitudes toward those whose lifestyle has brought about this doom of death. The attitude for some has been "They got what they deserve" or, in some circles, "They are receiving God's judgment for their sin." Statistics tell us that each year more and more people will be infected with the HIV virus. With this in mind, the church must work to avoid the prejudices that influence the decisions we will make concerning these people who are in the body of Christ. The following biblical responses need to be thought through in order for the church to respond in a mature fashion.

Someone might say, "Doesn't Paul confirm that AIDS is a judgment in Galatians 6:7–8? It says, 'Do not be deceived: God cannot be mocked.

A man reaps what he sows. The one who sows to please his sinful nature, from that nature will reap destruction; the one who sows to please the Spirit, from the Spirit will reap eternal life.'"

In chapter 5 of Galatians Paul lists the fruit of the flesh and the fruit of the Spirit. None of us are exempt from displaying the fruit of the flesh, the only difference is some are more noticeable than others. Yes, Jim reaped his condition from illicit sex, but the responsibility of the church is to care for and encourage him.

A major theme of Galatians is Paul's response to the Judiazers, the legalistic believers who tried to place all believers under the requirements of the Jewish law. Those who are unwilling to share in the burdens of others become like the Pharisees and place a heavier burden on others. Jim's lifestyle eventually caught up to him, but now his new life in Christ was transforming his inner man. To judge him now for his acts done while he was an unbeliever would place an even heavier burden on him and would also deny the power of the cross at work in his life.

John 4:7 and following vividly records Jesus' encounter with the Samaritan woman who was considered a social outcast by Jews and a moral outcast by her own people.

"When a Samaritan woman came to draw water, Jesus said to her, 'Will you give me a drink?' (His disciples had gone into town to buy food.) The Samaritan woman said to him, 'You are a Jew and I am a Samaritan woman. How can you ask me for a drink?' (For Jews do not associate with Samaritans.)"

In verses 16–18 we read, "He told her, 'Go call your husband and come back.' 'I have no husband,' she replied. Jesus said to her, 'You are right when you say you have no husband. The fact is, you have had five husbands, and the man you now have is not your husband. What you have said is quite true.'" But instead of condemning her, Jesus used the acknowledgment of her present situation to share with her the greater truth: the promised Messiah had come to bring the gift of living water to the spiritually thirsty.

One's deeds, sown in the flesh, will manifest themselves, if not here, then certainly in eternity. Our responsibility, however, is to show love and grace in the same way Jesus dealt with the Samaritan woman, the lepers, or the other outcasts of his day.

Suggested Approaches

In the beginning stages the pastor chose to protect Jim's confidentiality and as a result practiced the greatest happiness principle. He was a good shepherd to his flock and was able to communicate the facts at the appropriate times.

As time progressed and Jim's condition worsened, the pastor wisely chose to make an adjustment in how he communicated Jim and Sue's confidential dilemma. At first the pastor dealt solely with Jim and Sue. Over time the pastor confided in some couples who would surround Jim and Sue with strength and support. These factors eventually worked together and helped the church to grow.

As Jim's condition became apparent, the complete story needed to be told, and the congregation become aware of the situation. Kant's axiom of truth telling became the reality at this point in the process for the church. We can adjust the third quadrant and replace it with truth telling. When this is done, the judgment will change from protecting the congregation by withholding the facts to telling the truth and strengthening a community of believers by displaying concern and love. Telling the truth to the congregation eventually resulted in helping Sue work through the difficult times that followed.

Conclusion

The issue of AIDS crosses denominational barriers, ethnic diversity, and rural or urban centers. Getting past the initial negative response may be difficult for some because of the stereotypes associated with the illness. Shame, guilt, anger, love, concern, and isolation are emotions that can erupt in church members when confronted with someone with AIDS. In this case, Jim impacted many in his church because of his testimony and vibrant witness for Christ. He surrounded himself with strong believers who encouraged him and grew to understand the struggles of his life. The church rallied around him and prayed for him as they learned from his life. "Now the time has come for the church to climb off the fence, to stop taking pot-shots at the tip of the iceberg, the bit they see (erroneously) as consisting entirely of promiscuous homosexual men and drug addicts, and to start considering the whole picture: millions of men, women, children, and infants who are dying worldwide."[3] What will our response be?

Discussion Questions

- What type of involvement would an adult with AIDS have in your church?

- Knowing your congregation, how would you tell them that a member has the HIV virus?

- What level of confidentiality would you keep if someone asks you about an HIV-positive person?

- Make a list of the AIDS support groups in your area and have a representative from a group speak at your church.

CHAPTER FOUR

ORDAINED INFIDELITIES

THE PAST LIVES IN THE PRESENT

LEADERSHIP JOURNAL commissioned a poll to determine the scope of infidelity among pastors. The survey probed the frequency of behavior that pastors themselves feel is inappropriate. In the words of one respondent, "This is, by far, the greatest problem to deal with."[1]

Of the three hundred pastors who responded, 12 percent admitted to having sexual intercourse with persons other than their spouses since being in the ministry. Twenty-three percent responded to having done something that they felt was "sexually inappropriate" with persons other than their spouses. Eighteen percent confessed to other forms of sexual contact with persons other than their spouses since entering the ministry.[2]

As one pastor wrote, "This survey covers the greatest agonies of my life." If nothing else, it affirms once again the reality of temptation and the need to renew commitments to personal purity.[3]

The reality of infidelity is especially disheartening because the ministry is a calling, a unity that ends with one inappropriate act.

"Perhaps you can identify. Perhaps you have been there when a spiritual leader whom you put your confidence in fell into sexual sin. Maybe it was your pastor. Or maybe it was your best friend. Perhaps you went to college (or even seminary) together, or you had known each other since childhood. The awful news had come—your friend had been involved in sexual misconduct. The details held no interest. What remained so painful was the hurt you saw later in his eyes, the effect upon his whole body and soul. His very spirit ached so profoundly that you felt it. There is no way to relate to this, unless you've been there."[4] What follows is the story of two young pastors' relationship and how the action of one and the beliefs of the other were tested outside the seminary classroom.

Three stressful years of seminary education were coming to a close. Each student was anxiously waiting to hear from that special church that God had divinely chosen for him or her. How would His hand of providence reveal itself in their lives?

In those three years, lifetime relationships are planted, cultivated, and grown. Two friends, Steve and Joe, anticipated the day they would move and at the same time would be saddened by separation. When the day finally came, Steve went to a church on the West Coast while Joe took a church in the Midwest.

Time passed but they kept in touch. During their ministries each experienced diverse situations that tested their integrity. Steve and his family meshed well into their community and church home. The people loved the family's enthusiasm, servanthood, and commitment to Christ.

Joe wrestled with a young church and the dynamics of policy making, giving vision, and developing leaders. His ministry was marked by the death of his five-year-old son, who ran into the street chasing after a baseball and was struck by a car. Although the ministry grew, he and his wife continued to grieve over their loss. They seemed never to get over it. During those difficult days they communicated regularly with their best friends on the West Coast and even visited them to try to escape from their pain.

After seven fruitful years of ministry on the West Coast, Steve abruptly took a new position in another state, which made Joe wonder what had gone wrong. They continued to keep in touch. After a while, Joe forgot about Steve's sudden move and they made plans to see each other again.

One year later, while the two couples were on vacation together, Steve's wife tearfully told Joe's wife the reasons for their move.

Steve was a youth pastor who had made a tremendous impact on the teenagers as well as the people in the community. One of the youth sponsors was a woman who was having marital problems. Over time she became attracted to Steve and made herself available to him as much as possible. After all, he listened to her, comforted her, and seemed genuinely interested in her. The attention and self-esteem she lacked in her marriage Steve gave her. Her obvious affection appealed to Steve's ego. He flirted with her affection and soon found himself out of control.

First it was touching, then holding each other, then kissing, and complete infidelity occurred while they were on a youth retreat. Within six months she was in the process of a divorce. He became cold toward her; he could not shake what he had done. To make matters worse, she was his wife's best friend. When she wasn't with Steve, she would spend time with his wife.

The church continued to impact the community, and eventually the senior pastor was called to another area of ministry. The people in the church admired Steve, the youth pastor, for his preaching and people skills.

As a result, the search committee extended to Steve a call to be the senior pastor. When the former female youth sponsor heard about this, she issued an ultimatum to Steve. "If you take that position I will tell everyone what happened."

Steve was trapped. Fearing the worst, he eventually confessed to his wife the events that had transpired. She was devastated and angry and her trust had been betrayed.

As Steve's wife finished her story, she told her friend, "I wonder if I will ever be able to trust him again."

Joe held to extremely high pastoral standards. He believed infidelity to be one sin that disqualifies a person from pastoral ministry. Joe believed that Scripture is clear on what it is that qualifies one for pastoral ministry. He found no exception for what Paul has described as the criteria for an elder or pastor in the church. He believed that if you are a student of the Word you should know these things. After all, you don't need to be a Greek scholar to understand the passage in the pastoral epistles. First Timothy 4:12 provides a summary: "Set an example for the believers in speech, in life, in love, in faith and in purity." Titus 1:6–9 further adds, "An elder must be blameless, the husband of but one wife, a man whose children believe and are not open to the charge of being wild and disobedient. Since an overseer is entrusted with God's work, he must be blameless—not overbearing, not quick-tempered, not given to drunkenness, not violent, not pursuing dishonest gain. Rather he must be hospitable, one who loves what is good, who is self-controlled, upright, holy and disciplined. He must hold firmly to the trustworthy message as it has been taught, so that he can encourage others by sound doctrine and refute those who oppose it."

With these verses of Scripture weighing heavy on his conscience, who would Joe tell? His loyalties were tested in an area he never anticipated. Maybe Steve needed Joe's support rather than judgment.

What should he do? Encourage Steve to seek restoration? Tell the truth to the denomination's credentials committee? Pretend nothing ever happened?

The tension between right and wrong competes with loyalties, theory, and practice. The fine line between a cry for help and an honest evaluation often becomes fuzzy.

After all, Steve had spent so much time, energy, and resources getting a seminary education. If the truth were made public, how would his children understand the situation? What would they think of their dad? How would this impact their concept of the church and the pastorate? Besides, ministry was Steve's life; what else would he do?

Decision-Making Tower

Friendship, biblical principles, truth telling, compassion, and denial seem to stretch us at some point in our ministries. To one person this case appears to be cut-and-dried, for another it challenges his or her concept of love. For Joe it was too close to home. His loyalty to Steve and his family pierced his heart deeply. The beliefs he held to were put to their ultimate test. As we work through the Decision-Making Tower, I am sure you will find yourself identifying with one of the judgments (see fig. 4.1).

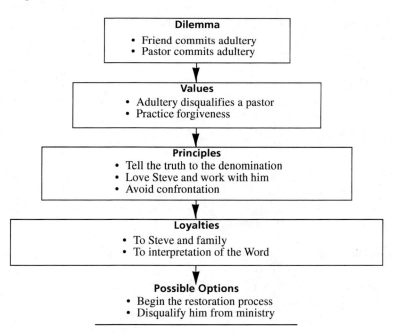

Dilemma
- Friend commits adultery
- Pastor commits adultery

Values
- Adultery disqualifies a pastor
- Practice forgiveness

Principles
- Tell the truth to the denomination
- Love Steve and work with him
- Avoid confrontation

Loyalties
- To Steve and family
- To interpretation of the Word

Possible Options
- Begin the restoration process
- Disqualify him from ministry

Figure 4.1

Ethical Guidelines

So what are our options and what do we need to keep in mind as we work through this all too familiar dilemma?

- Ignore the problem and hope it goes away.
- Inform the appropriate people and make it impossible for Steve to ever serve in another church.
- Pray for him.
- Publicly disgrace him and his family.
- Love him by disciplining him with the focus on restoration.

- Judge him according to the Scriptures in relationship to his office and disqualify him from ministry.

"Many churches exercise 'containment procedures' on the sexual affairs of church leaders, not only failing to inform the denominational hierarchy but also the next ministry to which the pastor or leader goes. A bargain is struck, 'You leave, and we will forget the whole matter.' A misapplication of confidentiality keeps the information under wraps and perpetuates the problem."[5]

The heart of the matter becomes the pain we all feel. We have all heard the saying, "The truth hurts." In cases like this I wish it only hurt one person, but the pain ripples like waves through many people's lives. The following personal ethical guidelines need to be considered:

- Confront the friend with the truth.
- Enlist the counsel of those who are not as close to the situation if the adulterer is a friend.
- Understand the difference between pastoral restoration and personal restoration.

Pastor are falling with increasing frequency. Seek out some friends who will let you peel off your mask. Don't be afraid to ask some tough questions. Listen to the advice of Solomon: "Above all else, guard your heart, for it is the wellspring of life."

Biblical Issues

No human being is exempt from the desires of the flesh, the greed for money, or the want of power. Yet pastors must adhere to a more "separate" standard. The pastoral ministry is a high calling. Some significant warnings shout out from the Scriptures:

Matthew 18:15–20 teaches that a sinning brother is to be (1) confronted, (2) reproved, and (3) excluded from the church if he refuses to repent.

Acts 5:1–11 illustrates (1) the seriousness of sin within the church, (2) the sensitivity of the Holy Spirit to sin, and (3) the quick judgment of God upon sin.

First Corinthians 5:1–5 teaches that in the event of persistent, unrepentant sin, the church is to (1) grieve, (2) deliberate, (3) judge the sin, and (4) exclude the unrepentant member.

First Thessalonians 5:14 commands us to warn the disobedient and the disorderly.

Second Thessalonians 3:6–15 teaches us to (1) warn the undisciplined brother and (2) withdraw from him.

First Timothy 5:20 tells us to rebuke persistent sin publicly.

Titus 1:13 says to severely reprove those who teach untruth.

Titus 3:10 commands us to withdraw from one who causes divisions, but only after adequate warning.

In these passages, God makes it clear that He intends the church to take corrective measures in the event its members persist in the practice of sin.[6]

There is no doubt that Scripture is clear on the steps that should be taken to correct sin and maintain the integrity of His bride the church. But the question remains, is the pastor who is called to be blameless, above reproach, a husband of one wife, and teachable, held to a different standard because of his office? Would one of your deacons or elders who fell because of immorality and then worked through the restoration process be restored to his position? Does it make a difference if the person is salaried or if he or she volunteers? Is a sexual sin any different than any other sin against the body, like drunkenness or drug abuse? My intent is not to present an exegetical exposé but to raise questions as we handle the text and dialogue within our personal theological frameworks.

The influence and position of the pastor cannot be denied. For the sake of the body and those who look to him, it is our responsibility to help him and his family in the restoration process.

Suggested Approaches

Assuming that the fallen pastor has expressed repentance and has broken off the sinful behavior that brought about his serious fall, restoration can be considered. Here are three common approaches to handle the problem of the fallen pastor:

1. Immediate restoration to pastoral office. "Immediate" is defined as fewer than twelve months after the sexual failure.
2. Future restoration to pastoral office after a period of time for counsel as well as family and personal recovery. The procedure varies from church to church, but generally one to three years elapses before the fallen pastor is restored to ministry.
3. Personal restoration of the fallen pastor but with no possibility for restoration to office.[7]

Let's begin by quickly dispelling one approach that has at times blurred our decision-making process. This is the idea that what we do is of greater benefit than who we are. In other words, we deny James 1:22 and forget that we are not only to be hearers of the Word but doers also. We are to walk our talk. Steve could have said to himself, *Just think of the impact I have had on these teenagers and adults in this community. If this comes out, how would I explain everything I have taught? They do not need to know this one mistake; more people will benefit if it is forgotten.* This attitude makes excuses to justify the actions. All that matters ultimately is that souls are won for Christ and the church is growing. According to Scripture no common-ground approach is justified, although the desire to rationalize sinful behavior is very strong. For some, rationalization is not only a matter of avoiding discipline or resignation, but one of preserving personal economics and pride.

A different approach was gnawing at Steve's friend Joe. In his reasoning he was trying to be sensitive to the idea of truth telling and practicing love. Somewhere in this complex situation, Joe was trying to find that place where he did not just forget about the sin but at the same time did not blow away Steve's career and family.

For the sake of all parties involved, confrontation by those who have an established relationship with the pastor in question is essential. Loyalty to Steve motivated Joe to pray more diligently for both of them. He discovered that Kant's axiom of always telling the truth needed to be tempered with the Judeo-Christian response of love. Issues of immorality damage the family deeper than most of us realize. A wife questions her loyalty and her self-image; she has had the privilege of being a pastor's wife. She has comforted, encouraged, and protected her husband from some of the wolves Satan has deployed to gnaw at him. It is to be hoped she has been on the inside instead of on the outside looking in. In the eternal scheme, there seems to be a sense of urgency for the church to impart to the erring pastor a difficult but loving approach for correction.

I remember when my mother had cancer. The doctors determined that an operation was necessary. To experience relief and live a longer life, she needed to go under the knife and then have extensive chemotherapy treatments. In similar fashion, moral failure requires us to wrestle with our pain in order to heal.

Conclusion

For some Christians, there are no gray areas. Every issue can be reduced to black and white. The ethics of life force us to make difficult decisions or to deny the consequences. When we apply the Word of God to every situation like a panacea, we neglect to be as compassionate as our Lord so vividly manifested for us when He fed the five thousand. He looked on them with compassion for they were like sheep without a shepherd. He then proceeded to feed them, teach them, and heal them.

The writer in Hebrews 12:11 says, "No discipline seems pleasant at the time, but painful. Later on, however, it produces a harvest of righteousness and peace for those who have been trained by it." For almost twenty years I have worked to cultivate a deep relationship with my wife. We regularly communicate, spend time together, discuss ministry, goof off, and replenish ourselves by reading and praying. We work on our relationship. Our two children consciously and unconsciously pick up their cues from dad and mom. Sometimes that kind of scrutiny can be pretty scary! If my marriage and family is falling apart, what good will I be to the flock I shepherd? A jaded past can raise its ugly head in different areas at different times. Not everyone understands our struggles.

Guard yourself against becoming another casualty. Seek outside help if you have to. We all hurt when another pastor falls. One seminary professor recently said, "Ten years ago I used to teach my classes that eight out of a hundred pastors will fall to sexual sins. Now I have to tell them sixteen out of a hundred will fall." If we look in the mirror and remember what we see, with God's grace, maybe we can lower that statistic.

Six months after moving, Steve resigned from the pastorate to seek help with some of the deep issues that were manifested in his behavior.

Discussion Questions

• What are you doing to cultivate your relationship with your spouse?

• Should a pastor be restored to ministry if he has fallen?

• Articulate a biblical position defending your answer.

• What help would you offer to Steve's family?

A TRAGEDY OF ERRORS

THERE IS A POPULAR STORY of how an Eskimo kills a wolf. The account is grisly, yet it offers fresh insight into the consuming, self-destructive nature of sin.

First the Eskimo coats his knife blade with animal blood and allows it to freeze. Then he adds another layer of blood, and another, until the blade is completely concealed by frozen blood.

Next the hunter fixes his knife in the ground with the blade up. When a wolf follows his sensitive nose to the source of the scent and discovers the bait he licks it, tasting the fresh-frozen blood. He begins to lick faster, more and more vigorously, lapping the blade until the keen edge is bare. Feverishly now, harder and harder the wolf licks the blade in the Arctic night. So great becomes his craving for the blood that the wolf does not notice the razor sharp sting of the naked blade on his tongue nor does he recognize the instant at which his insatiable thirst is being satisfied by his own warm blood. His carnivorous appetite just craves more— until the dawn finds him dead in the snow.

So, too, the minister who finds himself critically wounded in the service of the Savior because of a moral failure. In 1992, Rev. Truman Dollar resigned as senior pastor of the Temple Baptist Church. His resignation was a result of a personal indiscretion. In order to help in the personal restoration process of Rev. Dollar, a committee of pastors and laypeople were chosen. Dr. Ed Dobson of Calvary Church in Grand Rapids was one of the pastors. Here is the account of his perspective of the process.

The sanctuary of the Temple Baptist Church near Detroit is an imposing and intimidating structure. Built in the 1960s, it seats four thousand people. The church has a rich tradition in the independent Baptist movement, at the forefront of the evangelism, Sunday school, and church-growth movements of the twentieth century.

I had spoken there many times before on happier occasions. But on this Sunday as I sat on the platform, it was different. I tried to sing the hymns, but I cried. I tried to concentrate on the special music, but my attention was riveted on the family in the first row. They were clinging to each other as if afraid to let go. They looked out of place, even though they had been in the church for years.

I tried to smile at them, and they tried to smile back. But it was obvious to both of us that there was little to smile about.

Many in the choir had tears in their eyes. It was like a funeral service: everyone putting on the best front possible, yet feeling that at any moment his emotions could come unglued.

It might have been easier had I not been so close to the family in the front row. Truman Dollar was a mentor and a friend. When I was considering leaving Thomas Road Baptist Church in Lynchburg, Virginia, it was Truman who counseled me nearly every day. When I moved to Grand Rapids and needed advice in making decisions as a pastor, I turned to him.

Looking at him now from the pulpit, I could not believe he was about to resign as pastor. It all seemed so unreal. The events of the last week flooded my mind.

I answered the phone and in his resonant voice, Jerry Falwell, the man I had worked with for almost fifteen years, said, "What are you doing?"

"Nothing," I replied. "I had to answer the phone." We laughed. Jerry quickly got serious.

"Have you heard about Truman's situation?" Without waiting for an answer, he continued, "I just talked to Curt Wilson, the chairman of the Temple Baptist deacon board. Truman has had some problems and is going to resign. They wanted me to come and help, but my visibility would only hurt the situation. Since you have helped in these types of situations before, I suggested that he call you." He briefly described some of the problems and assured me of his prayer and support.

Shortly after I hung up the phone, it rang again.

"Dr. Dobson," the voice said, "Dr. Jerry Falwell suggested I call you to see if you could help us." Curt Wilson and I spent almost an hour on the phone.

He explained that two years ago, Truman's fifteen-year-old son had overheard him talking to a woman from their former church. The conversation contained inappropriate sexual content. The son, not knowing what to do, told the youth pastor what he heard, who in turn confronted Truman.

Truman admitted he had spoken inappropriately, asked forgiveness, and the matter seemed settled.

Now, two years later, that episode resurfaced, and the entire deacon board had been informed. After a lengthy and stormy meeting, the deacons concluded they should ask for Truman's resignation.

I didn't sleep much the night following that phone call. I was shocked, disappointed, and hurt. I knew this would be a long and difficult week. I wasn't sure what our own church board might think. I wasn't even sure I was capable of giving advice or leadership in this complex situation. I did decide, however, that I would not walk away from Truman. He had been my friend, was still my friend, and would always be my friend. Whether or not I got officially involved in the situation, I would still stand by his side.

Later Truman explained his situation to me. He said, "Looking back, my conversation with that woman was a fatal mistake. There were other people who could have listened. I said things that were inappropriate and wrong. I'm embarrassed and ashamed of what I said. I was neither unfaithful physically nor were we ever together. But with my suggestive language, I was clearly in sin. I still find it hard to talk about what I said to her."

It was during one of those conversations that his teenage son picked up another extension and listened in. He was shocked by what he heard.

Shortly thereafter, his son went on a youth retreat. He talked privately to the youth pastor about what he heard his dad say. When they came back from the retreat, the son and the youth pastor confronted Truman.

He reluctantly admitted he had said those things. They agreed that no one else needed to know about it.

But the secret between Truman Dollar and the youth pastor created intense pressure. Their relationship began to deteriorate. Truman recalled the events.

"When the youth pastor would do something poorly and I would talk to him about it, he would say, 'Well, I guess I am not the only person who has messed up.' As his performance slipped, I thought about firing him, but it was clear, at least to me, that he was holding our secret over my head. He repeatedly threatened me, and I knew he would go public."

In time, however, the youth pastor did confide in other staff members. The church had been incurring excessive long distance telephone charges, so Truman installed a device to log the numbers of all calls placed. Reviewing the log one month, the church staff noted the woman's number had been called from Truman's line. Assuming the conversations had resumed, the youth pastor told the whole story to some others.

One Sunday, right after the morning service, the staff members confronted Truman in his office with their accusations and documentation.

"What in fact had happened," said Truman, "is that the woman's husband had called when I was out. I returned the call and talked to him. I tried to present my side of things, but the staff members insisted the incident had not been handled properly two years before and now they wanted my immediate resignation.

"It did not take me long to discover that this confrontation involved more than a discussion of purity. It was a well-planned revolution, a palace coup. If I did not resign, they said they would make the matter public."

Truman later admitted to me that he was traumatized that afternoon, not thinking or acting logically after the painful confrontation by several staff members: "I was left alone in my office for a few minutes. My mind played tricks on me. I thought perhaps the damage done to my family and the church would be minimized if I were not alive.

"My youngest son's 30-30 deer rifle was in my office; a staff member had recently cleaned it for me. I took a soft-nosed shell from the case and nervously shoved it into the chamber. For a fleeting moment, I thought the easiest thing would be to end it all."[8]

That night Truman and Donna just wanted to disappear. "Our whole world had just caved in. We felt abandoned by both God and man. We were both stunned. Thirty years of ministry gone—no job, no security, no future."

I was beginning to sense that there was no simple, predictable strategy with which to respond to this situation. The damage had been done, and the best that we could do was exercise some sort of damage control. I identified four goals:

1. To ensure that Truman was treated with dignity. Even if he had done wrong, it wasn't right to stomp on him.
2. To help the church work through the shock and help the church see there was hope beyond this.
3. To communicate a biblical perspective. The whole church, and especially these people, needed to accept the biblical command to forgive.
4. To discourage the church from making hasty decisions. My goal was to help prevent the church from splitting.[9]

Decision-Making Tower

This case raises a number of key issues. An analysis could begin by identification of the decisions that were made. This much is central to the resignation in the case of Dollar: (1) Dollar had to make a decision who he would tell the truth to and how much of the truth he would share. (2) The youth pastor was put in a situation that provided leverage for his personal agenda and he chose not to disclose the truth. (3) Someone

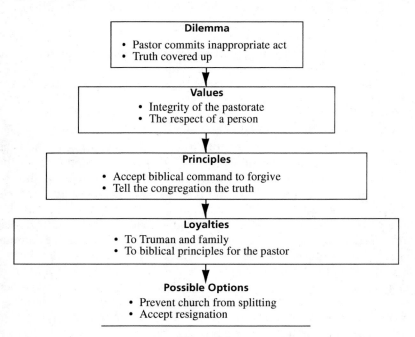

Figure 4.2

on the church board had to decide to request Dollar's resignation on the basis of secondhand information (see fig. 4.2).

Ethical Guidelines

This painfully common situation brings to bear a clash of values in the evangelical community. It would be easy if a standardized code of ethics detailed every possible misconduct of pastors. But this is unrealistic because rules can become legalistic and negate any practice of biblical love and mercy. Formerly there was no possibility of restoration when a church handled a pastor who was caught in sexual misconduct. The standards were not necessarily higher, but a greater consensus of what was and wasn't tolerated existed.

When applying ethical guidelines each of us needs to consider the following:

- Given your personality and theology, work out your thinking in this area.
- Does pastoral infidelity disqualify a pastoral from future ministry?
- What is the difference between personal and pastoral restoration?
- How will I communicate the facts to a congregation if called to do so?

The issues at stake involve principles, people, conscience, and theology. The cases we hear about sometimes confuse us. In the end they force us to work systematically through a process that we hope is best.

Biblical Issues

When considering biblical approaches, our minds immediately race to the most famous personal restoration in the Bible, King David. The Scriptures outline the tragic events of David's life. Standing on the rooftop he eyes Bathsheba. With telescopic vision he focuses in, and the unthinkable happens. Too bad Proverbs hadn't been written yet. He neglected to guard his heart. After his sin with Bathsheba, he remains king of Israel, but his conscience is plagued with guilt. About one year later, Nathan the prophet confronts him, and David writes the famous Psalm 51 describing his repentance. There was no time off the throne, no counseling to work through the deeper issues. He is back as if nothing happened. "David was restored to fellowship with God and his throne was not taken away. He remained a leader over all of Israel. This is strong evidence, proponents argue, that God have us keep a fallen minister in place if he immediately and openly repents and confesses his sexual sin."[10]

Conversely, Paul writes to Timothy that a pastor is to be above reproach, blameless. If this standard is violated and he is restored, how will it impact not only his future ministry, but the trust of his people? There is much more to pastoring than just teaching and preaching. The relationships we develop with our people and in our communities go deeper than we may comprehend.

When one man falls we all feel his pain. We hurt for his family. We look in the mirror and pray that God will give us wisdom in the choices we make and the situations we find ourselves in. Yes, he is a brother who is in need of personal restoration. He is not a disease that we should avoid but a soldier who is wounded and needs help in the healing process. The underlying tension focuses on our calling, our office, the laying on of hands for a specific purpose with a higher standard. These are the biblical issues we must wrestle with.

Suggested Approaches

The ethical decisions and choices made in this case are likely to be repeated in too many churches across the country. The various approaches to this dilemma may have even been the responses of your closest colleagues.

One might be strongly persuaded by Kant's ethic of truth telling. This appears to be Dollar's immediate response, without giving any thought to the position of the person to whom he disclosed such personal information. I suspect the guilt associated with his sexual inappropriateness made him vulnerable and eventually became his downfall. Dollar himself felt so humiliated he was overcome by the thought of checking out of life. His intensely turbulent emotions paralyzed him from considering other options. Should Dollar have requested a special meeting? For his sake and the protection of the youth pastor it seems this would have been appropriate. His desire to tell the truth would have been understood by different hearts and minds not necessarily as close to the situation.

Only the youth pastor "benefited" from Dollar's error of narrow disclosure. Dollar refused to tell anyone of the grasp—like the slow squeeze of a python—the youth pastor—and his own indiscretion—now had on him.

Consider Mill's principle. The youth pastor could have requested outside counsel from a neutral party. His actions would have been on behalf of Dollar and the whole church. Consider changing the third level in the Decision-Making Tower. If the greatest good for the greatest number of people had been implemented, Dollar, his family, and the church might have been spared from the events that followed. Often the bailout comes too late because there seem to be few options at the time.

Couple the youth pastor's immaturity with Kant's axiom of truth telling, right is always right and wrong is always wrong, and one has created an explosive situation.

Conclusion

What went wrong? Thirty years of ministry gone because of sin. The issue of infidelity continues to be discussed over and over. Are all sins created equal? Is the pastor just another person who wrestles with the tensions of the flesh? Does personal restoration mean pastoral restoration? Our passion for people and commitment to the Word create an uneasy match. It is easy to hold strongly to certain convictions on pastoral discipline and the steps involved—until the person is your best friend. I believe our primary concern needs to be restoring the fallen, caring for the family, and maintaining healthy communication with the church throughout the entire process. The longer a pastor is at a church, the more loyal the flock becomes. For some churches the hurt of losing a pastor is as traumatic as a divorce. They have grown to love him and he has grown to love them. He and his flock have grieved together over the loss of family members. He has married their children and dedicated their babies to the Lord. They love the pastor and the pastor's family. This sense of loyalty is one reason why some believers intentionally conclude that restoration means a return to ministry.

For all of us in ministry, the principles we teach to those preparing for marriage and the counseling we give when relationships are in crisis need to be practiced by us. We become so familiar with the importance of communicating but often are not home enough to practice it. We feel important as we mount the pulpit each Sunday because we make ourselves vulnerable to the transference of others. Oh, that we might pace ourselves, be on guard to those attacks, and make our spouses and families more than verbal priority. Preventive medicine will then be our best cure.

Discussion Questions

- What are you doing in your marriage that continues to strengthen and build the bonds of love?

- Dialogue with other colleagues about your biblical position of what would disqualify a pastor from ministry.

- What steps would you take in confronting another pastor concerning confirmed facts of an infidelity?

- Discuss what you consider to be sexual misconduct.

CHAPTER FIVE

CONVERSATIONS BEHIND CLOSED DOORS

SPEAKING THE TRUTH IN SAFETY

THE FOLLOWING STORY reveals the painful experience of a pastor who had to deal with lies, deception, and slander from a couple in his church who were acting out past sin and hurts.

Something was wrong with Faith Baptist Church. When I planted the church, fresh out of seminary, I was short on practical experience but long on enthusiasm. The congregation grew slowly but steadily from a handful of people to a morning attendance of 140.

But now, four years later, there was a deadly malaise of negative, critical attitudes seeping through the church. And it seemed centered in the Bilo family.

Claude Bilo, his wife, Vivian, and their two boys, Brad and Toby, had moved to town from out of state two years before. The Bilos joined the church and quickly became key leaders in our youth program. In a young church with many new believers, the Bilos were just the sort of Christians I needed. They had been believers for many years and were graduates of a Bible college. Even better, they had been involved in a new church in their previous community, so they were no strangers to church planting.

But our relationship began showing strain. I was not sure why. I assumed the problem was my pastoral inexperience. After all, they were both older than me, with more years in church work—a fact they had pointed out more than once.

I began calling Claude every week just to keep in touch. Claude was invariably polite, but he kept his distance.

My wife, Dionne, and I had Claude, Vivian, and the boys over for dinner. The evening was pleasant enough, but after they left, Dionne said to me, "Do you think we will ever move beyond chitchat with them? We don't have this problem with anyone else in the church."

I could only shrug my shoulders.

One Saturday morning John and Marge Kennedy came to see me. Their fifteen-year-old daughter Amber and the Bilos' sixteen-year-old son Brad had become sexually involved.

They were angry at both Brad and his parents, whom they felt granted unwise liberties at home.

I assured them I would try to help them and the Bilos through this together, without hurting the young people. Then I made an error. I mentioned that the board and I normally met for prayer on Sunday mornings before services, so I would enlist their help and prayer support, and we would work through this together. The Kennedys went their way, considerably more tranquil than when they came.

The next morning I told five members of our deacon board the story and asked for their prayers and counsel. Later, after the morning service, I took Claude aside.

"Claude," I said, "the Kennedys were in to see me yesterday about Brad and Amber. I told the board this morning so they could pray about the situation. I want you to know you have our full support." Claude looked stunned and then muttered a thank you.

That afternoon Claude called me at home. He informed me that he and Vivian were upset that I had so grossly mishandled the situation with Brad and Amber and demanded to see me that night. With stomach tightening, I agreed to see them after the evening service.

When I arrived they took turns attacking me, saying how wrong I was to tell the board about their son without getting their permission.

I learned some valuable lessons about discretion and timing. I mumbled my apology over and over and finally left, exhausted. At least the problem has faces, and I have apologized, I thought.

I went to work repairing the damage as best I could. I scrupulously avoided mentioning Brad and Amber to anyone else. The Kennedys, Bilos, and the board agreed to keep the matter confidential. Both families insisted the young people would not see each other again. I met separately with Amber and with Brad, and they were open to what I had to say and were repentant. Thankfully, Amber was not pregnant. I was only too glad to be finished with the issue.

Not long after, however, I began to hear from other church members comments like these: "Are the Bilos still upset with you about the thing with Brad and Amber?" "I guess you botched the deal with the Bilos, huh?" The source of the information was always Claude and Vivian. They had been furious about the possibility of other people in the church finding out, but they were the ones spreading the story!

"It feels like they're using this as a weapon," I told my wife one night.

Then Claude was elected to the board a few months later and used his position to take out his anger on me. Nearly everything I proposed, he opposed. Our minutes recorded many six-to-one votes.

After six months of frosty communication with the Bilos, my wife and I set up a meeting with them. They seemed eager to get together. We met at our home for dinner and spoke frankly about our damaged communication. Once again I apologized and asked for their forgiveness. We prayed together, and Claude hugged me as they left.

A while later another church member asked me, "Pastor, I don't understand why you never asked forgiveness for the situation with Brad and Amber."

From still another person, I heard that Claude had told the adult Sunday school class, "I'm not sure the pastor is good for this church. He holds a powerful sway over new Christians. I hope we don't have another Jim Jones on our hands."

At that point, I called Greg Bradley, the board chairman, and asked for his help. I said I had attempted private reconciliation with Claude and Vivian, but now I was afraid anything I said to them would be twisted and used against me.

The board met six times with Claude and Vivian and six times with me and Dionne to hear our differing versions of the problem. They concluded that Claude and Vivian were using slander and outright lies to force my resignation.

Eventually the board set up a special church meeting to recommend their dismissal and again talked with Claude and Vivian, urging them to repent.[1]

Decision-Making Tower

The fine line between confidentiality and the counsel of many can for some become the pan they unintentionally fry themselves in. The situation for this pastor seemed be a case of two teenagers going too far in their relationship, coupled with defensive and angry parents with a hidden agenda. In the pastor's mind the right thing to do was to enlist the help and prayer support of the leaders of the church. But what he encountered was an undercurrent that he was not prepared for even after apologizing and asking forgiveness. The analysis of the case will help us to understand the various positions (see fig. 5.1).

Ethical Guidelines

Today's pastor is confronted with many different personality types as well as with the wounds people carry around. The unresolved guilt, the need to be loved, anger, and a host of other emotions frequently are

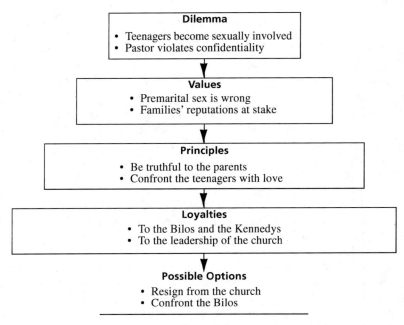

Figure 5.1

directed at pastors. Sometimes a woman feels madly in love with her pastor, but in reality she is not in love with him but with a persona of someone he represents to her. In the same way there are those who grow to despise pastors and either leave or make life very uncomfortable for them by the stress inflicted on their families. For some, pastors become a parent, the husband they wish they had, or that authority figure who hurt them sometime in their past. Our need to become students of ourselves is evident in this case. The Bilos, sometime in their past, had a problem with authority. Their manipulative passive-aggressive behavior constantly stirred the waters but their motivation never came to the surface.

The hard realities of the ministry constantly motivate us to look in the mirror. This is especially true as the baby boomers get older, and the church shifts its gears to meet the needs of Generation X. Here are some things we need to remember:

- Do your best to know your own personality style and learn to listen beyond words.
- Early in your ministry seek the counsel of someone in order to get a different read on situations.
- In situations like this, truth telling is much better than peacekeeping.

Above all else pray that God may give you wisdom and discernment as you shepherd the flock He has given you charge over.

Biblical Issues

Shepherding the flock doesn't change. The sheep keep bleating, listening to our instructions and following our footsteps. But there are those who never seem to be satisfied; the Pharisees and the Sadducees just don't go away. And we ask ourselves, how much is enough? How much love do I give to a couple such as the Bilos before I let them go? Where do I draw the line between love and discipline? How much do I write off as spiritual immaturity? When does it become a church matter?

If this couple was the only problem in the church some of us might say, "Let's have a party!" The church at Corinth wrestled with a host of issues, which Paul addressed in his letters. In 1 Corinthians 3:1–3 he writes, "Brothers, I could not address you as spiritual but as worldly— mere infants in Christ. I gave you milk, not solid food, for you were not yet ready for it. Indeed, you are still not ready. You are still worldly. For since there is jealousy and quarreling among you, are you not worldly? Are you not acting like mere men?" For some in the church, the problem seems to be they just don't know any better. The Bilo's troublemaking may have been a cry for help, a personality deficiency that needed some spiritual correction. I remember early in ministry wanting certain people to leave my congregation because I didn't like confrontation. I apologized more quickly than I should have. I would take responsibility for something that wasn't all my fault rather than dialogue with them and grow together. It takes a great deal of energy and a lot of self-confidence to tackle a dragon. But I am convinced if we desire our people to grow beyond troublemakers or mere babies in Christ then we need to help them digest solid food that nourishes them. Today, I am a little wiser because I have been crushed in the ministry. My own experiences have made me more sensitive to the sheep I watch over. I am more apt to meet with those who are dissatisfied and hear them out. I let them know what they say is important, but I also wedge the Word of God in our discussions. Our people need to know the body is made up of many parts. Just because God made one person a big toe and someone else an elbow doesn't mean some are less important.

In 1 Corinthians 12, Paul drives this point home to the Corinthians. Wake up! There is no room for heavy egos in the church. The body is made up of many parts. Some are eyes, some are hands; they are all important. This is the biblical issue that our people need to hear, and these are the issues that confront us. Our people have a desire to feel like they are special in the church. This is why there is such a loud cry for community in the church. Many look to the church to meet the needs left unmet from growing up in broken families. The healthy church is fitted and joined together so that the parts are functioning properly.

Suggested Approaches

This young pastor's inexperience seemed to be his strength and his weakness. Evident in this case is a Judeo-Christian ethic for displaying Christlike love. The pastor was not quick to judge the teenagers or "flog" them in front of the congregation. In fact, he was wise to seek the counsel of his deacon board—but perhaps not during a prayer meeting. He sought to handle the parents in the same way he handled the erring teenagers. But to his dismay, they had deeper issues that were not as easy to pull out. Hostility is something no pastor enjoys, particularly a pastor who is in his first church. Seeds of doubt begin to creep in and move the pastor toward shying away from other decisions for fear of the same thing happening.

If we consider this through the truth-telling principle of Kant, the pastor would have created more problems then he had already. The Bilos already felt there was a broken confidence. As a result, they used this as a doorway to transfer their anger toward the pastor. Truth telling can become callous. Applying Kant's principle, the church would feel the teenagers sinned and needed to repent before the congregation. This approach is like drilling a tooth without any Novocaine. We eventually fill the tooth, but with a tremendous amount of hurt and pain. Yet the situation of sexual activity needed to be addressed, particularly since it was brought to the pastor's attention by the parents of the girl.

What ethical principles can we draw from this? Would this be the best way to approach the situation? Due to the age of the girl and the nature of the offense, the church leadership would have to use more discernment in their actions. Scripture is clear that a church leader who has sinned should be brought before the congregation, but not a teenager who is already in an embarrassing situation. The more appropriate way to handle the situation would be a private meeting of the pastor and church leadership with the girl and her parents. In this way, the girl would not feel she was being put on trial, and love would have been shown to all parties involved.

But, we ask, was the young pastor afraid to approach the Bilos for fear of what they might say? Was he really protecting the innocent by just praying for them? Where were his loyalties? In the end, the situation became blurred because the Bilos had deeper issues with the pastor. By communicating and assessing the situation in an appropriate manner, the pastor's Judeo-Christian ethic worked and his care for the teenagers, their parents, and the church was manifested.

Conclusion

There once was a cheesemaker who mastered the craft of making the finest Swiss cheese. One day while making cheese he had an accident and lost his right thumb. The paramedics came and rushed him and the severed thumb to the hospital. He was immediately taken into emergency surgery to try to repair it, but to no avail. The thumb had been severed from the hand for too long and eventually had to be removed.

This put the cheesemaker in a dilemma. He was a master at making Swiss cheese but needed his right thumb. How could he do his normal functions? How could he write? He now realized how important his thumb was to the rest of his body. So he questioned the doctors and specialists. After much discussion they told him that in order to get a thumb back they would have to perform another special operation. They would have to remove his right big toe and place it on his hand. They talked some more and the man agreed. The operation was successful. The big toe took, followed by several plastic surgeries. The only way you would have known was if you knew the man. But something else happened as a result. The cheesemaker was now losing his balance. His right big toe helped him maintain his balance while he walked and worked. Going back to the doctors one more time they fitted the cheesemaker with a big-toe prosthesis. After this, he continued to make the finest cheese in the area.

This story brings to mind the need for the body of Christ to exercise the gifts God has endowed each believer with to edify, strengthen, and equip the church for service. Those with the gift of wisdom practice wisdom; those with mercy practice mercy; those with leadership lead. Especially in the decision-making process of the church, when the gifts of others are neglected the body of Christ will stumble, like the man who had no big toe because he needed a thumb.

We are all at different places in the journey toward Christlikeness. Some need encouragement, others need to be taught how to walk, others must be carried. All are important, even those parts that seem less honorable. The Bilos cared enough to get involved; they also needed someone to confront them on the baggage that the Enemy was using to blur their focus.

Discussion Questions

- What is your church's and your personal approach to a teenage couple caught in sexual involvement?

- How do you handle difficult people in your life?

- What is your church using to get people to understand how they fit in the body?

- Have you discovered your personality style and the people you need to surround yourself with?

<hr>

NOMINATING CHURCH OFFICERS

THE FOLLOWING STORY is played out over and over in those churches who choose new officers annually. How are we to interpret information concerning a potential candidate? How much should be said? Here is one dilemma that challenges wise decision making and keeping a confidence.

Thanksgiving had just passed at the Oxford Community Church. The twelve-member committee had just convened to begin putting a slate of officers together for the next church year. A list of church members was passed to each person on the nominating committee. Some time was spent praying for the guidance of the Holy Spirit and seeking God's will concerning those who would lead Oxford Church.

There was a time of silence as the members cautiously evaluated each potential name for the open positions.

"How about Jeff Smith for the position of elder?" asked Marilyn Guess. The chairperson wrote Jeff's name down along with others that would eventually go to the pastoral staff for review. Pastor Williams, who sat on the committee, thought Jeff Smith might make a splendid choice for elder. After all, Jeff had once pastored a church and his walk with the Lord seemed consistent.

In a few days the phone rang in Pastor Williams's office.

"Hello, Pastor Williams. This is Mary Jones. Pastor, I understand Jeff's name came up as a potential candidate for the office of elder at church."

"Yes," answered Pastor Williams.

"Pastor, has Jeff ever told you why he left the ministry ten years ago?"

"Why, no," answered Pastor Williams.

"You see, Pastor, I have never told anyone else this before but," silence hung for several moments, "you see Jeff has wrestled with homosexuality on and off for most of his life and has tested HIV positive. I know his life appears to be in order on the outside, and deep down Jeff would love to be an elder at Oxford but for the wrong reasons.

"You see, Pastor Williams, if you keep him on the slate I know you will have more difficult problems to deal with in a few years. Pastor, please do not tell anyone else. I hope I have made myself clear."

Pastor Williams hung up the phone, stunned by the conversation. Who would he tell? What would he say to the nominating committee about the reasons why Jeff's name should be taken off? People would begin to wonder. How come he never heard any of this before? Did Mary Jones have some personal agenda? Pastor Williams prayed and tried as hard as he could to be discerning.

Two days later at a staff meeting, Pastor Williams questioned his staff about their knowledge of Jeff Smith. He shared his conversation with Mary Jones and asked them not to repeat any of their discussion. In the back of his mind he wondered if he had broken his confidence with Mary. These were his colleagues in ministry; they needed to know, he thought. Without picking up the phone and talking to Jeff, Pastor Williams took Mary Jones's conversation to heart. For him it was a closed file. Jeff had a problem, Pastor Williams reasoned to himself. If he becomes an elder his problem will become my problem. In the wink of an eye there was no more discussion.

At the following nominating committee meeting Pastor Williams suggested Jeff Smith's name be taken from the slate. Several questioned him as to the decision. Pastor Williams guarded Mary's and Jeff's confidentiality, protecting not only them, but, in his mind, the church body as well.

Decision-Making Tower

Wow! Is it really that easy to prevent someone from becoming a leader in the church? What was really going on? We will never know for sure. Pastor Williams had perfected the art of protecting himself without processing the whole situation. I wonder if his leadership style would consider any other form of analysis? Let's look at some of our options (see fig. 5.2).

Ethical Guidelines

"This pastor's perplexing situation may be unique, but it raises a host of common questions and issues that pastors face. In each church, leaders must wrestle with how much to say—and leave unsaid—about current and former members.

"What happens, for example, when nominations for board positions roll around? How much can a pastor safely say about a potentially disruptive nominee?"[2] Whose "two cents" are worth a million dollars? How far do we go into someone's past?

Probably one of the most common areas in the church life that deals with confidentiality is in the area of nominating church officers. Some committees border on gossip, while others take on an "it's part of the territory" mind-set. I think for some churches nomination of officers resembles a supreme court appointment: leave no stone unturned.

After considering Pastor Williams's dilemma, several guidelines jump

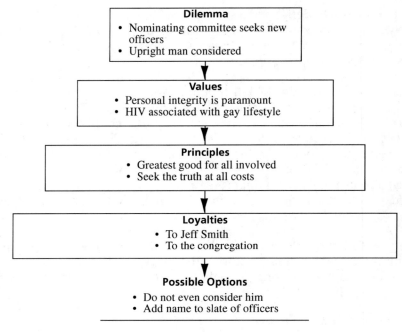

Figure 5.2

out at us. We will assume that his personality style is prone to avoiding conflict and that he is gullible to take people at their word instead of investigating the truth.

Most of us are in ministry because we feel God has burdened us with a call. Just as there are many different types of churches and communities, there are many types of pastors. There are leaders, healers, helpers, teachers, people pastors, and even those wondering who they are and why they are in ministry. Pastor Williams appears to be someone who is a teacher, given to the preservation of the Word. This is of utmost importance. Maybe you can relate to him, but, at the same time, make sure you still hear the bleating of your sheep: know them and know yourself. If you are an introvert who dreads the thought of potlucks or home visitation and pastor a small church, I can guarantee you experience extra stress. If this is you, find someone who loves people and develop a relationship with him. Use the members of the body to complement your personal style.

Pastor Williams did little to communicate with Jeff Smith. After receiving the phone call from Mary Jones he resolved that Jeff was not the right man. In the same way he exegetes the Word, he should have dug into Jeff Smith's life. Not only would this have been helpful to him, but it also would have confirmed or disqualified his conversation with Mary. Seeking the truth as the pastor of the church is vital. Officer nominees are the future leaders of the church and people you might desire to disciple. With Jeff's case in mind, let us work to do the following:

- Understand your personality style and how it blends with others.
- Get the facts from the horse's mouth, this way there will be no surprises later.
- Pray for discernment regarding how much you say.

Armed with understanding, the facts, and prayer, you will provide an example of a healthy leader who seeks to be used by God while bringing out the best in others.

Biblical Issues

As I reflect on the story of Jeff Smith, I am drawn to the book of Philemon. Before meeting Paul, Onesimus was a slave to Philemon. Evidently he'd had enough of servanthood and wanted to experience the good life. He stole some money from Philemon to fund his trip and split the scene. Not only was Onesimus a fugitive slave, he also was a thief. If caught his punishment could be death. In God's sovereignty, Onesimus met Paul, who shared the Gospel with him. He immediately believed, and he experienced a transformed life. Paul enjoyed having Onesimus around, but he also knew the ethical thing to do was to send him back. So he wrote his letter to Philemon urging him to take Onesimus back as a brother in Christ.

> Therefore, although in Christ I could be bold and order you to do what you ought to do, yet I appeal to you on the basis of love. I then, as Paul—an old man and now also a prisoner of Christ Jesus—I appeal to you for my son Onesimus, who became my son while I was in chains. Formerly he was useless to you, but now he has become useful both to you and to me. (Philem. 8–11)

Paul knew where Onesimus came from and practiced Christ's model of love and forgiveness. Had Pastor Williams gotten to know Jeff Smith in the same way Paul knew Onesimus things may have been different. The truth is, we are all fugitives from our pasts. The issue therefore becomes how we administer the love and forgiveness of Christ when it comes to church officers. Does our past have to haunt the present? Sometimes yes and sometimes no.

So how much information should Pastor Williams divulge in order for a nominating committee to remove a member's name from the slate? I believe this is where we need to have a good understanding of the characteristics of an elder and deacon, as listed in the pastoral epistles. Some of those characteristics listed are more difficult than others to discern. For example, some churches will not even consider a divorced man as an elder or deacon no matter what the circumstances, while other churches take each case on an individual basis. But what about someone who has had a history of homosexuality or alcoholism in the past? Will this prohibit him or her from serving in a specific capacity? These are the issues we need to work through ahead of time. We will never know all the specifics, but to prepare a strategy for approaching these situations will help us down the road.

How would we handle it when someone intercedes on another's behalf? There are times in ministry when God sends angels who give us information that will preserve our integrity as shepherds of the flock and keep us from undue conflict. Let us consider the character of Abigail, who was married to Nabal. She overheard what he did to King David and realized not only Nabal's life, but her own was at stake. By God's grace and wisdom she discerned the situation and met David before the worst happened.

First Samuel 25:23–28 reveals her heart.

> When Abigail saw David, she quickly got off her donkey and bowed down before David with her face to the ground. She fell at his feet and said: "My lord, let the blame be on me alone. Please let your servant speak to you; hear what your servant has to say. May my lord pay no attention to that wicked man Nabal. He is just like his name—his name is Fool, and folly goes with him. But as for me, your servant, I did not see the men my master sent.
>
> "Now since the LORD has kept you, my master, from bloodshed and from avenging yourself with your own hands, as surely as the LORD lives and as you live, may your enemies and all who intend to harm my master be like Nabal. And let this gift, which your servant has brought to my master, be given to the men who follow you. Please forgive your servant's offense, for the LORD will certainly make a lasting dynasty for my master, because he fights the LORD's battles. Let no wrongdoing be found in you as long as you live."

Abigail was not selfish in her assessment of the situation. She desired the greatest good for the most people. Even though Nabal was a fool, she was still a faithful wife. Even though David was angry, she had the wisdom to defuse the situation and at the same time help David understand the importance of his integrity as king. Tempering honesty with wisdom brought out the best in this situation. May our prayers in these matters be similar to those of Solomon, who asked for wisdom.

Suggested Approaches

One approach might be to bring Jeff Smith before the elders or deacons for a preliminary interview. Be up-front with him so that everyone is well informed and comfortable. If he loves the Lord and has proven gifts, discuss his past lifestyle and how it flows with the biblical character of an elder in the church. In so doing, he might disqualify himself or give clarification on his situation. Truth telling in a smaller sphere is critical for all parties involved. Jeff's honesty will also validate or invalidate the conversation Pastor Williams had with Mary Jones. Instead of being afraid of how someone will feel, seek out the facts. Too often, decisions pertaining to key church members are made in the church parking lot or in a "smoke-filled" room.

Another way to address the situation has nothing to do with Jeff Smith. Every year, church nominating committees meet to put a slate of officers together for the annual meeting. When it comes to our elders or leaders of the church we need to be practicing Paul's admonition in 2 Timothy 2:2: "And the things you have heard me say in the presence of many witnesses entrust to reliable men who will also be qualified to teach others." The apostle Paul discipled Timothy and had a strong relationship with him. Brothers in the ministry, find the Timothys in your church and begin marking their lives. Seek those faithful servants who have confirmed gifts and meet the qualifications for deacons and elders. If we start doing this, the situations like Pastor Williams' will decrease dramatically.

Conclusion

The good news is that in many churches nominations come around only once a year. The bad news is if we haven't been sensitive to the flock, we will have to live with certain decisions for a year or more. The case of Pastor Williams stresses the importance for us to know our congregation.

Jesus spent time with His disciples modeling servanthood, teaching, and instilling in them His master plan of evangelism, even though they were unaware of that until the Holy Spirit came. The disciples were unschooled men who often wondered what the Master was talking about when He referred to the future kingdom. After Pentecost they were bold, confident, and able to articulate the Gospel. What the Master had taught them began to make sense.

Our people are looking for us to lead them on their journeys toward

Christlikeness. This involves training, discernment, and much prayer. As Howard Hendricks has stressed, we need to have Timothys in our lives, those whose lives we are marking for the kingdom.

> Again, the key is to build relationships with people. By regularly making contact with people and spending time with them, you will discover where they are. You will be able to learn their need. You will keep in touch. You will accurately evaluate their effectiveness. In short, you will find it much easier to personalize everything you do.
>
> People grow in relationships. In relationships where there is trust, there can be vulnerability. There can be a willingness to admit and explore change. There can be the support and follow-through needed to sustain growth. So the writer of Hebrews urges us to "spur one another on toward love and good deeds" (Hebrews 10:24). God understands the impact one person can have upon another. He made that point a long time ago. In Proverbs He wrote the book on the role of relationships in personal growth. "As iron sharpens iron, so one man sharpens another" (22:17). Without contact there can be no sharpening.[3]

The church today longs for relationships because so many have come from fractured families. In Chicago, for example, there are many people who are transplants from other parts of the country because of job transfers. They seek community through the church in order to replace what they had. Some come with confirmed gifts and a high level of maturity, others desire to be used by God in servant roles. When relationships are highlighted, situations like Pastor Williams's will be minimal.

Discussion Questions

- What events in a member's past will disqualify him/her from running for a particular church office?

- How would you work with a nominating committee divided on nonessential issues?

- What approach would you take after talking with Mary Jones if you were Pastor Williams?

- Develop some guidelines or ground rules for a nominating committee so that the integrity of individuals is maintained.

CHAPTER SIX

ANSWERING CRIES FOR HELP

WHEN CURIOSITY BECOMES A HEARTACHE

OUR YOUTH ARE THE NEXT leaders of the church. How we disciple and teach them we hope will give them the tools for making wise decisions in the future. The following story reminds us that teenagers require lots of love and support when the weight of the world seems to be squeezing them.

Megan did not seem herself lately. The bubbly high school junior seemed lethargic, almost apathetic to the events of the evening.

"Not feeling well?" I asked in passing.

"I wish that was all it was," she answered.

I could tell by the tone of her voice something was wrong. It was only September, and she refused to take off her coat during the two-hour youth group meeting.

Megan's dad was the church chairperson. He and I had developed a close relationship over the three years I had been at Hope Church. I respected his leadership and willing ear as I sought to bring about healthy changes in the youth group, so naturally I had some loyalty to Megan. There were times when I felt I gave her extra attention, and tonight was one of those nights when I felt like probing a little deeper.

"Hey Megan, how about if we have a Coke tomorrow after school at McDonald's?" I asked.

Reluctantly she nodded an OK.

I talked with my wife, Julia, about the situation; we prayed and went to bed. I did not get much sleep that night. Thoughts raced through my mind.

I got to McDonald's a half hour early, sipping down a large coffee, praying, and thinking. I saw Megan walk in the door and asked her to get whatever she wanted, it was on me. After she got her food, we made our way back to the booth.

I broke the silence with a question.

"So, Megan, what has been troubling you lately?"

There was more silence as she played with her French fries.

"Pastor Steve," she said as her lip began to quiver. "You know Dave in the youth group?"

"Sure, he moved here from Texas about six months ago."

"Remember right after he moved here we dated for a couple months over the summer?"

"Yes," I replied trying to pull the words out of her mouth. Her eyes started to water and soon big tears began to roll down her cheeks.

"Megan, what is it?" I said.

Her voice went to a whisper.

"Pastor Steve, one night he took me to a movie and afterward we drove to Chippewa Park and [she paused], he raped me."

I felt like I had just been shot. Feelings of anger came over me, mixed with concern. What would I do now? I thought of Megan's dad and how he would react. I was not sure I was ready for this one. *Why me, Lord? You know I cannot stand conflict. Everything seemed to be going so well and now this! What can I do now? This is going to get pretty ugly!*

I just listened as Megan retold the events of the evening, sobbing as she relived the pain.

I was not even sure if I should get the local authorities involved. Was Megan looking to me for guidance? I was just doing what I learned from youth group seminars. Taking kids out in order to get to know them. I wasn't ready for this.

"I am afraid to tell my folks for fear of what they'll do," she said. "I don't want them to think it was my fault."

"Why do you feel that way?" I asked.

"They never wanted me to go out with him in the first place. They questioned his character. They told me it was something they could just tell about him. I didn't understand what they meant. Now I do. I am so ashamed."

I prayed for Megan and asked God to help me do the right thing. I wished I had a handbook to go to. But I knew it wouldn't be that easy.

Decision-Making Tower

Steve's story may be your dilemma. The feelings that stir within when we hear of teenagers who are violated move us to tears, anger, or action. "Not all secrets are created equal. The tensions of confidentiality increase, I believe, as the information revealed becomes more serious. How the counselee communicates such information often determines how serious the situation is."[1]

Not knowing how to process his feelings and afraid of the potential conflict that would follow, Steve began avoiding Megan. Over the next

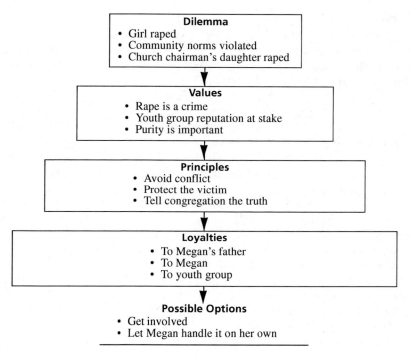

Figure 6.1

year, her attendance at youth group was very sporadic. Steve just kept doing ministry and eventually moved on to another church after only three years. Even though he was miles away, the thought of Megan's dilemma haunted him.

Should someone be told? Are other girls in the youth group in imminent danger of Dave's sexually aggressive behavior? If Pastor Steve did get involved would truth telling become his priority for protecting Megan and her family from further emotional distress?

Pastor Steve displays what is blatantly characteristic of one who lets his personality style dictate the decision-making process. Depending on your personality, ignoring conflict is easily supported from a biblical perspective. Some might say, "Let go and let God work it all out. He will work the situation out in His perfect timing." But this mind-set rationalizes our fear and freezes us in a state of denial. A teenager has been severely hurt. What will we do? What steps can we take?

Why get involved when it might stir the waters; after all everything is going just fine. As for Steve, other things were going through his mind. Let us see how his dilemma might look sorted out through the Decision-Making Tower (see fig. 6.1).

Ethical Guidelines

Faced with an ethical dilemma, Pastor Steve began processing his responsibility and actions. He felt like someone had just said "check" in a game of chess. His ethical framework left him little room to maneuver. He had always believed God's love covered everything. As a result, he did not say a word, mostly because he hated conflict.

"I can think of few, if any, aspects of youth ministry that require greater sensitivity. A friendship is a fragile commodity, a commodity vital to teenagers. Doing what friendship requires will not always be understood or appreciated by kids—or by their parents! But if a young person's life is spared or if a family is restored in the process, it will be worth whatever price we must pay."[2]

For Steve this was his worst nightmare. Accompanying his personality style was his hesitancy to seek advice or counsel. Steve had injected the Judeo-Christian love ethic with a theological virus known as *antinomianism*. The basic premise of antinomianism is that we love God and do what the heart wants. The misconception is that if we love God we will inevitably do what is right. In other words, it will all work out in the end, just pray a little harder. This reduces Christian love to a series of acts. There is no room for this ethic in Megan's case. She has been violated. She is scared. She feels she has nowhere to turn.

Here are some practical suggestions to help you be prepared:

* Read some good books on the subject of rape in order to be better informed.
* Develop a relationship with a community social worker and discuss the "what ifs."
* Develop a plan in your ministry for something like this.
  Who would you go to first?
  What steps would you follow?
  How would you help the victim?
  What information is confidential?

Rape is a serious crime. The pain is felt for a lifetime. If you don't know how to handle the situation, find someone who does. Sometime down the road of life, especially after marriage, this issue will surface in a woman's life if she has not been helped early on, and then her pain is experienced all over again. Only now others are involved. If this crisis happens in your ministry, stay focused on who and what is important.

Biblical Issues

As I think about this topic my fingers turn the pages of my Bible to the story of Tamar in 2 Samuel 13. Verse 1 tells us, "In the course of time,

Amnon son of David fell in love with Tamar, the beautiful sister of Absalom son of David." The story goes on to tell us how Amnon became frustrated even to the point of illness because he could not get what he wanted from Tamar. After pretending to be ill and having Tamar take care of him, he raped her. She pleaded with him to let her go but the text says in verse 14, "He refused to listen to her, and since he was stronger than she, he raped her." After he had filled his sensual desires, the passage goes on, "Then Amnon hated her with intense hatred. In fact, he hated her more than he had loved her. Amnon said to her, 'Get up and get out!'"

When David heard of this he was furious. Yet there is nothing recorded in Scripture that says he took recourse for Amnon's actions. How could he? After all, he just had to look in the mirror and remember his own strong desire to have Bethsheba and the actions that followed. Deep in his heart he knew he could not do anything.

But Amnon's crime did not go unnoticed. The rage and embarrassment Tamar's brothers felt, their love for their sister, and their family pride, stretched beyond their capacity for love and forgiveness and led them to act in the most brutal way possible. The laws back then dealt severely with those who committed rape, but they also placed a heavy burden on the victim. Tamar, in the Old Testament, was damned by the law because her half brother raped her. She was a desolate woman.

Some in our day desire the same severe punishment for rapists as Amnon received. Those who feel this way have a difficult time working through this moral issue because their loyalties or love for the victim dictate their decisions.

Rape should hold a severe penalty. This is a crime that is different from burglary. You cannot give back virginity or dignity. You cannot undo the psychological trauma that is inflicted on the victim of rape. The horror and pain may go with a woman to the grave.

In the Old Testament, the Law reigned, but in the New Testament isn't love supposed to reign supreme? Isn't Jesus' admonition to love unconditionally? In Matthew 5:43–45, Jesus in the Sermon on the Mount says, "You have heard that it was said, 'Love your neighbor and hate your enemy.' But I tell you: Love your enemies and pray for those who persecute you, that you may be sons of your Father in heaven. He causes his sun to rise on the evil and the good, and sends rain on the righteous and the unrighteous."

Jesus adds in Matthew 6:14, "For if you forgive men when they sin against you, your heavenly Father will also forgive you." Humanly speaking, it is impossible to forgive a rapist. This is why it is so necessary to work through the pain and accept God's grace in order that by His Holy Spirit a victim will have the capacity to forgive.

"Forgiveness does not mean that what happened to you did not matter or hurt. Forgiving never means excusing or condoning what the rapist did. It does not mean that the offender should not suffer the consequences of his actions under the law. Forgiving means that you actively choose to give up your grudge in spite of how much you have been hurt. Forgiving means that you release the power the offense has over your life and use it for more constructive purposes."[3]

The tension that exists between pain and forgiveness is difficult to accept. "It is easy for you to say I should forgive because you don't understand what it is like." Many of us don't understand, but, in the same way, we have difficulty comprehending Christ's death on the cross. His sacrifice gives us a model for forgiveness.

Suggested Approaches

Consider a more appropriate response to Pastor Steve's dilemma. First, we have already identified that Steve's personality bent is to avoid conflict. In order to compensate for this weakness he should immediately confer with the senior pastor regarding a course of action and get Megan's parents involved. This is one dilemma where practicing a Kantian truth ethic will move things in a healthy direction. Considering Steve's personality, the best way to implement this approach is through someone else. Steve will be buffered from the personal stress that accompanies conflict resolution. Because Megan is a minor, he has a responsibility to maintain a certain level of confidentiality, but at the same time he needs to get her parents involved as quickly as possible. This approach would be focused on Dave and his actions. He would then be under the scrutiny of the church and of the law.

Another approach is to love Megan in such a way that she is supported without feeling at fault. When Megan was talking with Steve, she worried that her parents would think it was her fault. This is a common fear among rape victims. Assure her that she was not deserving of any such action.

Though Megan's experience was months in the past, here are some steps you should understand when dealing with a rape victim shortly after the crime.

> It is important for every woman to be prepared for the possibility of rape. How adequately she responds to the crisis of a sexual attack will be proportionate to how she has been trained to respond. In order of importance, here are the steps:
>
> 1. Get her to a safe place and contact a family member or a friend she can trust, or call your local rape crisis center for support and information.
> 2. Call the police.
> 3. Get medical attention as soon as possible. Unless you need

immediate first aid, do not change anything concerning your appearance. Do not shower, bathe, douche, wash your hands, brush your teeth, comb your hair, eat or drink anything, or use the toilet if at all possible. Don't change or destroy clothing or bedding. Resist the urge to straighten any disorder or clean up any mess."[4]

A Judeo-Christian love ethic not only seeks to console the hurting but also practices tough love to those who need to be disciplined. Dave must get help for his anger and aggression. This will provide the best support for Megan as you work to begin the healing process and bring to light similar acts that Dave might have done in Texas.

Finally, confront Dave! This will achieve the greatest good for all parties involved. I would also advise Steve to meet with a juvenile officer and/or social worker in order to get a better handle on the severity of the crime as well as to get an outsider's perspective. If you ignore the situation, it will become like a splinter and eventually get infected. The church needs to get involved. Jesus did!

Megan came to Pastor Steve because she trusted him to do the right thing. He responded in a style that offered no alternatives. The outcome was a devastated and guilt-ridden teenager.

Conclusion

"Many people view rape as a punishment for sin or as a natural consequence of a victim's wrongdoing. Women have been blamed for their victimization for reasons including: dyeing their hair, failing a biology class, not attending church Sunday nights, and driving the wrong kind of car. People have difficulty believing that painful experiences such as rape happen without provocation, so they create a reason or a higher purpose for their own peace of mind."[5]

Our society is challenging the pastorate from every angle. We study theology, develop our preaching skills, attend Promise Keepers, and go to prayer summits. Then, when that which we thought would never happens knocks on our door, let us not catch ourselves saying, "I didn't know what to do." Learn the steps to take if a rape victim comes to you. Develop a network of resource people who are trained in this area. Be a model for conveying Christ's love. Pastors like Steve need to make sure they are acting wisely and responsibly in their daily involvement with young people and their parents.

Discussion Questions

- Discuss with a group of professionals the steps involved in helping a rape victim.

- Get to know the laws of your state for the crime of rape.

- Ask an attorney what confidentiality privileges you may or may not have.

- Discuss how you might biblically discipline a teenager or adult who has committed a rape.

LIFE OR DEATH: YOU MAKE THE CALL

SOMETIMES THE MINISTER will take an oath of silence in order to listen to important information. Then there are times when keeping a confidence will mean the difference between life and death. The following story challenges what we say and what we do in a life-or-death decision.

Pastor Jim Sudberry of the Mount Vernon Bible Church was fresh out of seminary. During his first year of ministry he held to the principle of absolute confidentiality, promising not to tell anyone the secrets people divulged. He never dreamed of practicing duplicity, but after one desperate phone call with Judy, a woman he had counseled on several occasions over the past year about serious depression, he found out that keeping quiet about some things could mean becoming an unwilling accomplice in the destruction of a family.

During that desperate phone conversation with Judy, he sensed he was not making any headway with her. The minutes ticked by as Pastor Sudberry went over again for the third time a responsible interpretation of her perceived problem. He shared Scripture with her, encouraged her to get involved in one of the church's twelve-step programs, and prayed with her. He knew Judy had no money, so referring her to a Christian counselor was out of the question. Besides, the nearest available counselor was a one-hour drive away. Pastor Sudberry recognized Judy as someone known in pastoral circles as an EGR, Extra Grace Required.

After listening to Pastor Sudberry, Judy continued on. "I can't handle it anymore. My life is worthless. I wish I was never born. I'm just a throwaway person. I always have been, so I might as well get on with it. I'll see you Pastor. Thanks for your help." There was a pause in their conversation. "Ever since I was a little girl, nobody has ever loved me. I guess that's because I'm just a bad person. I don't blame my parents, or anyone else, as a matter of fact, for not loving me." He could hear the receiver of the telephone fall to the floor and then get picked up.

Pastor Sudberry heard the crackling in her voice and a strange noise that he later guessed to be the "pop" of a prescription bottle in the background.

"Judy, don't!" he yelled in the phone. "Let me come over and we'll talk."

"No! Stay away!" she screamed as she slammed down the phone. He called right back, but there was no answer. Thoughts raced through his mind.

Did she have the right to die without interference? Should he divulge her troubles to others who could help? Was this her way of getting the attention she so desperately wanted?

He did not pause to debate the ethics of confidentiality. He remembered that when he was a teenager growing up in an affluent suburb, his best friend told him how he wanted to die. Jim was too young to take him seriously—only to find out from his mom the next morning his friend was gone—forever! Those memories of his friend haunted him. Now it was Judy.

He immediately called Frank Warton, a church member who lived near Judy, and explained the situation.

"Frank, this is Pastor Sudberry. I need your help. Just listen and do everything I tell you."

In a matter of thirty seconds he told Frank the dilemma. "If she doesn't answer the door and it's locked, kick it in. Trust me. We have got to save her," he told Frank.

Pastor Sudberry jumped in his car and raced to her house, just like when he was taking his wife, Andrea, to the hospital when she gave birth to their daughter.

He arrived as the ambulance was pulling away. Frank had kicked the door in and found Judy unconscious, curled in the fetal position on the floor next to the sofa, an empty bottle of prescription medication near her.

Fortunately he got there in time. Later the hospital confirmed she had taken a deadly dose of painkillers. When she regained consciousness, she asked Pastor Sudberry, "I thought things told to a pastor were kept in complete confidence. How could you tell Frank what I was doing? Why didn't you just let me go?"

He smiled and answered, "Sometimes there are things in life more important than keeping a person's confidentiality. Sometimes it just boils down to life-and-death issues!" He looked at Judy as tears began to flow from his eyes. "Judy your life is important to me, the church, and especially to God. We want you to know we love you. Please accept our love."

Decision-Making Tower

The trust factor between pastor and people is very important. Oftentimes we are called upon to guide our people like professional counselors. We pray for wisdom, try to learn good listening skills, and help our people with biblical principles that will guide their lives. Among all the other hats we wear is this one that we need to carefully consider. I say this because we live in a very litigious society. Here is what Pastor Sudberry faces (see fig. 6.2).

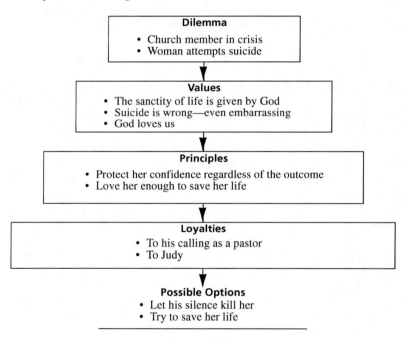

Figure 6.2

Ethical Guidelines

In the past, a pastor was seen as a partner in a trusting relationship. Now we are seen as professional counselors. In the eyes of the law we wear a different hat. The case that made national headlines several years ago involving Pastor John MacArthur confirms this. A church member who had experienced suicidal tendencies and emotional instability in his past was seeing a pastor for counseling. After one of the counseling sessions, he took his own life. His parents proceeded to sue the church. Grace Community Church was eventually acquitted of any wrongdoing but only after spending thousands of dollars and coming under the scrutiny of the press. There are times when we need to refer counseling cases to those who are professionally trained so that we do not become victims of our own best intentions.

The case with Pastor Sudberry represents a healthy approach to moral decision making. Sudberry clearly stated early in his ministry that the framework he works with is an absolute approach to keeping the truth confidential. I commend him for his firm convictions and willingness to adjust when the situation dictates.

In one sense Pastor Sudberry reveals the tension many ministers face between belief and behavior. To those who are hard-liners, Pastor Sudberry would appear to be inconsistent or hypocritical in his ethical beliefs. In principle, what is absolute for one case should be maintained for all cases. In considering ethical decisions it is important to remember no decision is made separate from our personalities, our culture, and all of our personal life experiences. This is why some of us are more compassionate than others. God has wired us differently, and this is evident in our moral and ethical decision making. So I continue to encourage you to seek out those who see life from other perspectives. The body of Christ will be better off because of it. This is the difference between knowledge and wisdom.

- Think about what principles you might compromise in the case of life and death.
- Gain some insight into the warning signs of those who have suicidal tendencies.
- Research with your insurance agent the parameters of your liability coverage.

The ethical dilemma for Pastor Sudberry could have been a difficult one had he not considered Judy's life of greater value. He remembered his friend who took his life at a young age. As a boy, Pastor Sudberry had no thought of what this might mean to him later. Now in the ministry, his feelings were replaced by actions. A decision on his part to maintain strict confidentiality could have haunted him for the rest of his life.

Biblical Issues

"There is little in the Bible concerning the morality of suicide. Indeed, the word 'suicide' (self-murder) does not appear. There certainly are examples (without comment on the moral nature of the act), as in the cases of Saul and his armor-bearer (1 Sam. 31:4–5), Ahithophel (2 Sam. 17:23), and Zimri (1 Kings 16:18). In the New Testament, the only example is that of Judas Iscariot (Matt. 27:5). The death of Samson (Judg. 16:28–31) may possibly be seen as a heroic suicide, although it is possible that Samson did not primarily will his own death, but accepted it as the unavoidable consequence of his actions."[6]

The discussion concerning suicide goes back to the early church. Augustine came to understand suicide as murder and thus violating the sixth commandment, "Thou shall not murder" (KJV). Even in the Westminster Larger Catechism suicide is forbidden because it challenges the sixth commandment. Others, however, challenged Augustine's view as a placing of limits upon the grace of God.

Many Christians who hold that God is sovereign in all of life conclude that He is the giver and taker of life. Solomon wrote in Ecclesiastes 3:1, "There is a time for everything, and a season for every activity under heaven: a time to be born and a time to die." Therefore, suicide is a challenge to the sovereignty of God. Many argue taking your own life is an offense to God. The discussion continues, does man have a free will to choose life and if so then does he have the option to end it?[7]

> The Christian perspective shaped the historical position of the West. Christians rejected the Stoic notion that the option of suicide was an important element of freedom. It was not until David Hume's (1711–1776) famous counterargument [that the Christian perspective] met with serious challenge. Hume's argument responds to each point of this tradition. He claimed that suicide is not an offense to God, since God's concern is only in maintaining the regular order of nature. The community's legitimate expectations toward an individual are reciprocal, and an individual is no more sinning against them by suicide than by emigration.
>
> While Immanuel Kant (1720–1804) reaffirmed the strict prohibition on suicide, current secular thought seems more drawn to Hume's view that suicide can, at times, be morally acceptable.[8]

The issue continues to be, how valuable is life and who decides when to die? Jesus said, He came to give life. How unfortunate when we hear of believers who, having experienced emotional overload, hopelessness, extreme depression, or loneliness, have silently or violently ended their lives. The biblical issues we wrestle with will continue to be discussed. Our challenge is to present the church as a safe place, a community where love is dispensed and egos are shelved. When asked, Why have You come? Jesus replied, To heal the sick and downtrodden. His compassion gave meaning and hope to a confused and lost people. Hope and healing are the real issues.

Suggested Approaches

So what ethical principle guided Pastor Sudberry to change his strongly held ethic? Pastor Sudberry recognized that he would be able to help Judy if he sought her greatest good. His approach was not to condemn or theologize Judy's situation but to try to help her understand her dilemma and give her an outlet for her emotional stress. "The potential suicide is already suffering from a heavy burden of punishing feelings. One who speaks about suicide as an immoral act will not only block the possibility of further communication, but may actually contribute and advance the individual's present sense of discouragement and depression. For the suicidal person, self-destruction is not a theological issue; it is the result of unbearable emotional stress."[9]

The healthiest approach for Pastor Sudberry is loving and informed aftercare. When Judy comes home from the hospital, she will still be wrestling with her issues of low self-worth and the inability to accept love. I would suggest he find a spiritual mother for Judy who will disciple her and show her love. I would also strongly encourage Judy to join one of the church's small groups. Her attempted suicide did not seem to be caused by a chemical imbalance but by a lonely heart. There are so many like Judy in the church today who cope with life in various ways. The difference is they do it in secret: promiscuity, homosexuality, drugs, alcohol, work, and so on. These hurting people all have one thing in common—the need to numb the pain inside.

Conclusion

"We can all bring something to the moment of crisis. This is portrayed most poignantly in Thornton Wilder's 'The Bridge of San Luis Rey' when the bridge collapses and plunges the persons crossing it to their deaths. In the attempt to discover what it was in each person's life that brought him or her to the ill-fated bridge of self-destruction, Wilder enunciated one certain truth: 'There is a land of the living and a land of the dead and the bridge is love—the only survival, the only meaning.' For it is the death of love that evokes the love of death."[10]

As we gain more of an understanding of Christ's love for our lives, then and only then will we be more open to share what He has given us. When Jesus conversed with the woman at the well in John 4, He offered her living water so that she would never be thirsty again. Even though she understood him to mean physical water, His words penetrated her heart. Here was a woman looking for love and security. One husband after another probably used her to fulfill his selfish desires. Her longing was never satisfied until Christ came along and showed her a more excellent way. This is the mandate of the church. The pain and trauma of those who consider suicide won't go away. The unique design of the

Master Creator calls us to minister to the hearts, souls, and minds of those we shepherd. One doesn't have to look very far to understand this. The increase of teenage suicides hurts all of us. Yet, there is hope! Next time you get together with your pastor friends, trade the names of agencies (Christian and secular) in your areas that will give you help before you face this crisis.[11]

Discussion Questions

- Is pastoral counseling considered equivalent to professional counseling in regard to confidentiality?

- Were there any options that Pastor Sudberry could have considered as he cared for Judy?

- In a case like this, does the value of life supersede confidentiality? Can you support your answer with any biblical principles?

- What advice would you have given to Judy?

CHAPTER SEVEN

FUMBLING WITH FIGURES

MAKING A BAD INVESTMENT

FOR MOST CHURCHES, the issue of money seems to be one area where trusting God is a constant but trusting in your own hunches can be disastrous. The following case can be replayed over and over in many churches. Only the dollar amount will change. The dilemmas created by the misuse of money can test how a church loves or disciplines. Let's see how one church handles such a crisis.

Walter Gregg did not suspect anything was wrong at first. All he knew was that when he and the church chairperson authorized payments to the contractor who was building the new educational wing for Garrison Avenue Methodist, church treasurer Fred Akerman seemed reluctant to write the checks. Two weeks after one major payment was due, the check still had not been written.

When the contractor called to complain, Walter phoned Fred, a stockbroker, at his office to ask what had happened to the check.

"I know we are a little overdue, Pastor," Fred said. "I will get it out. I'm running a little behind."

"We've got an obligation to pay bills on time," said Walter. "It's part of our Christian testimony."

The next thing Walter knew, the phone rang again and the board chairman was on the line. He said Fred had just called asking him to get the pastor off his back about the payments.

"He says the money is tied up in CDs," the chairperson explained. "If we withdraw it now, it will cost us an interest penalty. Is there any way we can hold off for two more weeks until the CDs mature?"

Walter pointed out the check was already two weeks overdue. He wondered silently why Fred had not told him about the CDs, but in the end he agreed to ask the contractor for an extension. The contractor was not happy about the delay. He had just paid his workers, and this put him in a cash-flow bind; but "since you are a church, I guess we can hold things together for two more weeks. But we definitely need the money then."

Two weeks later, on a Tuesday morning, Walter got a call from Everett Hinson, a church member and vice president of the bank where the church kept its accounts.

"Walt, I think we've got a problem," he said, with his voice serious. "Fred Akerman and I need to talk with you. And you better get the board chairperson in on this, too."

Walter could not imagine what had happened, but he called the chairperson. Two hours later, the four men were seated around the table in Walter's office. Everett began.

"Fred told me something today that I insisted he tell you immediately. Fred?"

Fred sat staring at the floor, and when he spoke, his voice slightly shook. "Two months ago, I heard about a great opportunity, a new company that was looking for investors. It was a sure bet. If I worked things right, I figured I could pay off the entire cost of the church's construction. I took the $182,000 in the building fund and invested it in the company's stock. It should have tripled in value within a couple months—we could have had half a million to pay off our construction. It was a terrible mistake. Yesterday I found out the company declared bankruptcy."

Walter felt his stomach getting queasy. "How much did we lose?"

"We lost it all," said Fred. "We may have a few hundred dollars from recent offerings in the building fund, but the $182,000 is gone. I'm sorry. It was bad judgment on my part."

Bad judgment! Walter wanted to scream. *How dare you take the entire building fund without telling anyone and invest it in some shady deal? Do you know what you have done to us? We owe the contractor an overdue $100,000, we have got nothing to pay it with, and the building is barely half done. You have just crippled us.*

Instead, Walter said nothing, groping for words. The room was silent. No one had any answers.

Finally he said, "This is too much to digest right now. Let's get the board together tonight, and in the meantime, let us pray for wisdom and resiliency, and maybe a miracle."

After Fred left, Walter got more details from Everett. Since building funds required two signatures, apparently Fred had been able to transfer funds to another church account that required only one. Everett had only heard about it that morning when Fred came in asking for a loan, intending to borrow money personally to reinvest and try to recover his losses. Everett eventually got the story out of him and demanded he tell the pastor right away.

"Even if he had made a killing on the market, how do we know he would have returned the money to the church?" Everett asked. "He sure was slick in the way he secretly juggled funds to get them under his sole control."

Walter just shrugged. "We are not judges of anyone's motives. Only God can do that." Privately he shared Everett's suspicions.

That night, Walter was amazed and pleased at the way the board responded. Yes, they were shocked. Yes, they were outraged. Yes, they were worried. But their focus was, What should Christians do in this situation? Their immediate concern was the overdue $100,000. All twelve board members agreed to borrow money and cash in savings accounts, whatever it took to pay the contractor. They would worry about the longer-range effects later.

They approached several other families in the church, and people responded by putting second mortgages on their homes and giving money saved for children's education or their own retirement. By Friday, Walter gave the contractor a check for $100,000.

The second concern was what to do with Fred. The board agreed that he should step down immediately as treasurer. But they did not want to press legal charges against him.

"The church is not in the business of putting people in prison," said one board member. "We are in the redemptive business."

Several people asked, "Is he sorry for what he did or sorry he was caught?"

In the end, however, the board identified three options: 1) skinning Fred alive and pressing legal charges, 2) officially forgiving but continuing to hold him personally accountable, or 3) forgiving and taking steps to develop a normal relationship.

The board agreed that the church's responsibility was to forgive, even though Fred's repentance left something to be desired.[1]

Decision-Making Tower

This is one situation that could have gone either way. The board at Garrison Avenue church was very focused in how they handled the situation. Their main concern was to maintain integrity by paying the contractor as quickly as possible. They were also aware of their options in dealing with Fred. If the board held to a strong Kantian principle in quadrant three, the outcome would have been different. We can notice how balanced the leadership was as we chart their course through the Decision-Making Tower and see how they came to their judgment (see fig. 7.1).

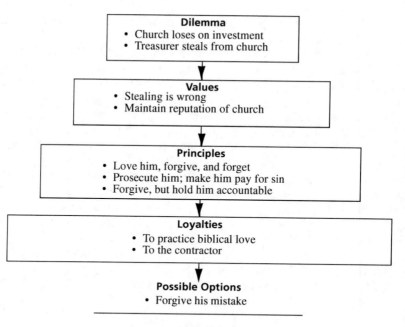

Figure 7.1

Ethical Guidelines

What type of ethical statement was the board of Garrison Avenue Methodist making to the congregation? The fact that Fred just gave away $182,000 would not go over well in any context. To whom is moral duty owed? to the parishioners of the church? to the contractor? to the Lord? The church board practiced a strong Judeo-Christian love ethic. We might ask, Is this principle applied in matters of the church that deal with personal sins that affect the body of Christ also? If so, how is discipline applied?

Here are some guidelines that might help prevent such a crisis:

- Consider placing financial limits on accounts that require one signature.
- Regularly audit how funds are being spent or transferred in-house.
- Let it be known that no one is above financial accountability, not even pastors.

The board might also articulate some guidelines for church discipline. Is discipline reserved for those who only commit moral failures, or does it apply in circumstances like this? If so, what type of discipline is necessary?

Garrison Avenue Methodist chose to settle the matter in the least disruptive way, which proved necessary to solve the short-term problem. But do the long-term results become more damaging in the areas of integrity, anger, and bitterness?

Biblical Issues

This is a story that scares pastors and church boards, and it occurs often. One member of the board stated his position of a strong love ethic: "The church is not in the business of putting people in prison. We are in the redemptive business." This is someone with great compassion. But what is the church to do?

As we analyze the situation we quickly are made aware of our position on right and wrong. God forgives, but man is still held accountable for his actions. Didn't Paul say in Galatians 6:7, "A man reaps what he sows." In the same way there are consequences to our actions in the physical world. Those consequences are visible in a person's life and in the church. The biblical issues at stake sometimes rest with how strong our convictions are and to what degree have we received God's grace in our own lives.

In the Old Testament the laws concerning theft were very clear.

> If a man steals an ox or a sheep and slaughters it or sells it, he must pay back five head of cattle for the ox and four sheep for the sheep. . . . A thief must certainly make restitution, but if he has nothing, he must be sold to pay for his theft. (Exod. 22:1, 3)

The principle of the law stresses the need for restitution. We may not find the law in Exodus binding for today, but we must come to terms with balancing forgiveness and restitution.

> The LORD said to Moses: "If anyone sins and is unfaithful to the LORD by deceiving his neighbor about something entrusted to him or left in his care or stolen, or if he cheats him, or if he finds lost property and lies about it, or if he swears falsely, or if he commits any such sin that people may do—when he thus sins and becomes guilty, he must return what he has stolen or taken by extortion, or what was entrusted to him, or the lost property he found, or whatever it was he swore falsely about. He must make restitution in full, add a fifth of the value to it and give it all to the owner on the day he presents his guilt offering." (Lev. 6:1–6)

Even during the early days of the nation of Israel there was fraud, robbery, and deception. Do the Scriptures give a strong case for restitution on the part of an erring or deceiving church member, one who, like Judas, was entrusted to manage the finances? Fred is ultimately accountable to the Lord, but what about the body of believers who elected him and trusted him? Does he owe them something other than repentance?

Some might argue that the church did the right thing. Our responsibility on this side of the Cross is to practice love and forgiveness. After all, Jesus paid the ultimate price for our sins. Let's consider the parable of forgiveness in Matthew 18:23–35.

> Therefore, the kingdom of heaven is like a king who wanted to settle accounts with his servants. As he began the settlement, a man who owed him ten talents was brought to him. Since he was not able to pay, the master ordered that he and his wife and his children and all that he had be sold to repay the debt.
>
> The servant fell on his knees before him. "Be patient with me," he begged, "and I will pay back everything." The servant's master took pity on him, canceled his debt and let him go.
>
> But when the servant went out, he found one of his fellow servants who owed him a hundred denarii. He grabbed him and began to choke him. "Pay back what you owe me!" he demanded. His fellow servant fell to his knees and begged him, "Be patient with me and I will pay you back."
>
> But he refused. Instead, he went off and had the man thrown into prison until he could pay the debt. When the other servants saw what had happened, they were greatly distressed and went and told their master everything that had happened.
>
> Then the master called the servant in. "You wicked servant," he said, "I canceled all that debt of yours because you begged me to. Shouldn't you have had mercy on your fellow servant just as I had on you?" In anger his master turned him over to the jailors to be tortured, until he should pay back all he owed.
>
> This is how my heavenly Father will treat each of you unless you forgive your brother from your heart.

Suggested Approaches

In this case we notice the board identified three options: (1) "skinning Fred alive" and pressing legal charges, (2) officially forgiving but continuing to hold him personally accountable, or (3) forgiving and taking steps to develop a normal relationship.

The first option of pressing legal charges would have demonstrated a Kantian ethic. There would be no compromising on Fred's behalf. This is clearly a case of wrongdoing and must be dealt with accordingly. What would have been the outcome if the board at Garrison Avenue Methodist practiced a Kantian ethic? Fred definitely would have been held accountable because he chose to deceive the pastor and the board. Fred's investment was on behalf of the church, but who is to say, if the company did strike it big, that he would have given everything to the church since he had done everything surreptitiously? A demand for restitution is the approach some churches have taken as the only way to confront a church member in a sin of this kind.

The second option of officially forgiving Fred, but continuing to hold him personally responsible, would lean toward Mill's principle. The greatest good is for the people. Fred blew it, but instead of nailing him to the wall, just make him pay it back. In so doing, things will proceed on schedule and he will have learned his lesson.

Yet, Fred's act of repentance seemed lame to some. If not holding Fred accountable for the whole amount, the board would require an agreement for restitution of a portion, say, fifty percent of the amount he lost. The church would still be involved. This would be an appropriate act because the church would understand what Paul said in 1 Corinthians 12:26: "If one part suffers, every part suffers with it; if one part is honored, every part rejoices with it." Although Fred clearly made a poor decision, he is still part of the body of Christ at Garrison.

The third option, forgiving and taking steps to develop a normal relationship, clearly displays a strong bond of love on the part of the church. But, we need to ask, when is love tough? And how much does love allow before discipline is necessary? Even the writer of Hebrews wrote that the Lord disciplines those He loves.

Conclusion

Striking a balance between restitution and forgiveness is not always easy. The personalities of those in leadership, the health of the church, and church priorities all come to bear in situations like this. What would have happened if Garrison Avenue Methodist wasn't able to come through in quickly raising the $100,000 necessary for the payment? What responsibility does the church have in auditing its financial accounts? I believe this is one area where the church gives an extra amount of grace. Not wanting to take their members to court, practicing forgiveness, and maintaining their pride all factor into the dynamic. As pastors we need to be aware of how our church handles its finances. My advice is to avoid getting involved in counting money, making transactions, or anything else that may place you in a compromising situation. Whether you are in a large church or a small church, the temptation is too great and the price is not worth it.

When Scripture tells us that Christ's love covers a multitude of sins, does it include deception that leaves a church financially crippled? Even when Joseph's brothers sold him for twenty pieces of silver it was meant for evil, but in the final analysis God meant it for good. The Lord does have the power to forgive, but how that is seen by those on the outside could present problems later on for Garrison Church.

Discussion Questions

- Is the church responsible for their volunteers' decisions if they are officers in the church?

- Should the church do background checks on those handling money?

- What would you have done differently if you were the pastor of this church?

- What type of restitution, if any, would you seek?

STUNNED BY AN INSIDE JOB

IN THE EARLY EIGHTIES WHEN I was in seminary, I was taught not to discuss my salary to avoid developing a reputation as someone who is money hungry. Yet for many pastors, the average salary today is far too modest. This tension can create a rationale to find other ways to compensate a personal financial shortfall. The following story reveals just how that type of behavior can be justified.

As the limousine pulled away from the gravesite it seemed like a bad nightmare for Denise Abbot and her two children. Just last week they were celebrating three years of ministry at the Crossroads Community Church. Her late husband, Tim, was the pastor, and finally, after the long-awaited finish of a building program, it looked like the church was headed in the right direction. But tragedy struck when Tim died in a car accident. The Abbots lived in the church parsonage, but soon that would change. They were both in their late twenties, and neither one had thought to plan for a death. Their salary was so small that several years earlier they had cashed in Tim's life insurance policy, trusting that God would take care of them. They agreed that when their finances were in better shape they would purchase a new policy. Denise was still numb from the events of the week and had given little thought to her financial future. All she knew was ministry.

The church took care of the Abbots for several months until they called a new pastor. It was then that Denise and her children had to move out and she had to find employment. In their community was a large well-to-do Presbyterian church that was looking for a secretary. Denise had secretarial skills, and her knowledge of ministry made a good fit for the position. She was hired and began working. Her days were filled with recollections of life with Tim at Crossroads Community Church. In fact, there were times when she felt like the pastor's wife all over again. Because of her position she was privy to information many of the members never knew. She never overstepped her boundaries and maintained a high level of trust. As a result, the pastor gave her more and more responsibilities.

A little over a year had passed. The children were involved in more and more activities, Denise had recently purchased a home, and, within the month, a new car. Her payments were within her allotted budget and she managed well. Then some unexpected repairs began to squeeze her. The furnace had gone out just before Thanksgiving. Living in the north pressured her to replace it immediately. Christmas came, and everyone celebrated the birth of the Savior. One thing about Denise—she was very generous in giving gifts. A couple of major credit cards came in very handy during the holidays. The cold of January froze the pipes in her laundry room, causing them to burst. The water damage and plumbing repair began to stress Denise. She had maxed out her credit cards as well as her home equity loan. The refrigerator didn't seem as full any more. She did the best she could to hide her anxiety from her children.

The spring concert came at the Presbyterian church and with it a special offering. On Monday the pastor gave Denise the offering and asked her to count it out and make the deposit. For some reason it needed to go in the bank right away instead of in the safe after it was counted by the finance committee. Denise separated and counted the checks, stamping each one "For Deposit Only." She placed the checks in one envelope and then proceeded to count the cash, placing it in a separate envelope. She had just finished counting the cash and had written down the checks on the deposit slip when the phone rang for her. Jimmy, her youngest, had taken ill in school. Denise put the two envelopes in her purse and quickly drove to school to pick up Jimmy. He was running a fever and was vomiting. Her attention was focused on getting him comfortable and taking the necessary steps for his recovery.

Two days later while she was digging in her purse she pulled out the envelope with the checks inside and deposited them. In all the distraction she had forgotten about the envelope with the cash. The next week Jimmy asked his mom if she had any gum. Denise always kept gum in her purse so she dumped it on the kitchen table hoping to find just one stick. She gave Jimmy the gum and, in shock, realized she hadn't deposited the cash from two weeks before. No one had said anything. She told the kids she had to run some errands and drove off in the car. She was on her way to the bank when she pulled over and thought, *It sure would be nice to fill up the refrigerator for the weekend. I will only use $100, and I'll pay it back. After all, I see how that church spends money. Here I am a widow. Doesn't the Bible say they are to take care of people like me? No one in the church has gone through the tough times Tim and I went through during those early days at Crossroads. Maybe this is just a gift from God. Anyway, they won't miss the money. Thanks, Lord. This will sure take the edge off my bill situation and feed us for a couple weeks.*

She drove to the grocery store and spent $150 on groceries. Another week went by, and still no one said a word about the money. Denise bought another $150 worth of groceries. Over the course of two months she spent the entire $600 in the envelope on groceries for her family. At first she felt a little guilty, but after awhile it was just another way the church was helping her out.

The extra money came in handy for Denise—so much, in fact, that she persuaded the pastor to let her count the offerings from every Sunday service. Her persuasive style convinced him it was the most efficient way to get the money to the bank and lighten the finance-committee load. During the first month she was a saint. Not one penny fell into her purse. As the temptation grew greater and greater, Denise found herself slipping ten and twenty dollar bills in her purse. Not even she knew how much money she was taking. During this time some people began to think it was not a good idea for one person to count the money. Unknown to Denise, a counting committee began counting the money Sunday night before she counted it on Monday morning. The first few weeks there seemed to be some discrepancies between twenty and fifty dollars. As the weeks continued and the errors remained some began to suspect Denise of wrongdoing. Although not verbally confronting her, the counting committee began to place decoys in the count. About this time Denise's mother was stricken with cancer, and she began taking more and more time off. Even though she was their prime suspect, no one wanted to confront her because of the failing health of her mother. Within a few months she sold her home and moved to take care of her mother.

Shortly after moving, her mother died and Denise became the secretary at her childhood church. She liked her job, but the church paid her substandard wages. Underneath she missed the extra spending money she had grown accustomed to. Soon, in her winsome way, she persuaded the pastor to let her count the Sunday offering. Even though she counted it with the other secretaries, Denise had a way of pulling out twenty, thirty, and even fifty dollars a week. The treasurer began to suspect something was wrong when the special offering that usually averaged $5,000 only came up as $4,000. He wasn't quite sure who it was but he was going to get to the bottom of this. One thing was for sure, wrong was wrong and needed to be punished—no matter what or who! Sure enough, on a Sunday in May, after some marked bills were placed in the offering, Denise was caught stealing. The investigation that followed revealed she had stolen at least $7,000 from the church.

At a special meeting the pastor opted for Denise to resign, but the board held firm. She was to be made an example of. Their understanding of Scripture was an eye for an eye. In an overwhelming decision the board voted to press charges against Denise. Eventually she was convicted and sentenced to spend six months in jail as well as pay back what she owed the church. During this time her children were sent to foster homes. Upon release Denise vowed she would never set foot in a church again.

Decision-Making Tower

Unlike the previous case, this one causes us to look at the issue of stealing and deception through a different lens. Isn't it interesting that Denise eventually took a position at her home church, the place where you would think love and forgiveness would be evident, especially since she was one of their own members. Our decision-making analysis is somewhat similar to that for Fred, the difference being a very strong desire for justice to prevail. Old Testament law set the precedent in Denise's case. We can also begin to understand more vividly how different personality types are integrated into the understanding of the Bible. For some of the board members who judged Denise, there were very few options to choose from (see fig. 7.2).

Ethical Guidelines

As followers of Jesus Christ, we must ultimately ask ourselves, what do we value the most? If unquestionable truth is our ultimate value, then there will be those who are swallowed up in the wake of our edicts. I am not talking about the truth in regard to the essentials of the faith, but those dilemmas, like Denise's, that could be judged either way: in love or truth. If love is to prevail, how will we balance the teachings of Jesus and the consequences of the sin?

"Ethics become an issue when what we value the most is threatened, and we must make the difficult decision of sacrificing our principles or our possessions. Ultimately, ethics are an issue of trust, a matter of which provider we will count on, mammon or God. Ethics demand a choice between masters, and the choice must be an absolute and consistent one because we cannot serve two masters—we must trust one or the other;

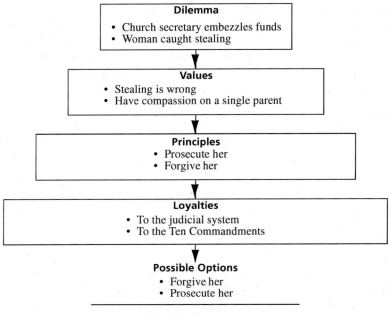

Figure 7.2

we cannot trust both, and whichever one we choose to trust replaces the other."[2]

While working on a graduate degree at Wheaton College, I worked full time for Boise Cascade Office Products. After my first year I wrestled with the whole money issue. I was making a good living but felt called into ministry. I realized if I started to climb the corporate ladder the money would only get better. During my second year, a war was raging over which master I was serving. My focus was blurred. After working there for four years, I learned much about the marketplace and the importance of working to live instead of living to work. My eternal perspective forced me to think of the decision I was making over the long haul. We need to come to terms with our own personal ethic on finances. When I took my first church in 1983, my total salary package was $8,500 per year. I paid my own taxes, rent, utilities, you name it. I learned what it meant to trust God. No, I wouldn't want to go through those days again. Studies have shown most pastors are underpaid and overstressed. As a result, the tendency to rationalize the personal spending of church money can become a greater temptation. Be careful or you might find yourself like Denise, a case study in someone's book. Here are some things we need to consider:

- Incorporate a financial skills ministry in your church.

- Review your accounting structure to make sure there are checks and balances.
- Establish a fellowship fund to help those who have legitimate needs.
- Make sure you have someone you can talk to about finances.

Some in church-leadership positions find it easier to press charges on financial issues then practice biblical discipline in other areas such as immorality, gossip, and so forth.

Biblical Issues

Several issues surface immediately as we think through Denise's dilemma.

The eighth commandment clearly states, "You shall not steal." There was no doubt that she was stealing. Yet in her mind it was compensation for her low pay. Paul writes in Ephesians 4:28, "He who has been stealing must steal no longer, but must work, doing something useful with his own hands, that he may have something to share with those in need."

We conclude that stealing is wrong not only from a biblical perspective, but also by law. If a person is caught stealing from a bank they would be prosecuted. Is there any difference? Some might argue no. Think back on the story in Acts 5 of Ananias and Sapphira. They deceived the church by holding back a portion of the money from their property. Isn't this stealing? In Acts 5:3, Peter says, "Ananias, how is it that Satan has so filled your heart that you have lied to the Holy Spirit and have kept for yourself some of the money you received for the land?" And then the ultimate judgment—death. According to the leadership of the church, Denise needed to be held accountable for her actions.

On the other hand, Paul writes to the church in Corinth that we are not to take Christian brothers and sisters to court. Denise was not only the secretary, but a member of the church. Paul was encouraging members of the congregation to settle their differences in a biblically appropriate manner within the church. But where and how does a church decide inappropriate behavior in the area of finances? What would have been the outcome if the leadership had selected a special team to investigate the situation? They may have discovered that Denise was under financial pressure because she was underpaid. They may have also recognized the church could have reviewed its counting procedures to prevent placing someone in a potentially compromising situation. In so doing they may have changed their counting practices.

Finally, the church could have recognized Denise's difficult situation. The loss of her husband and mother added extra stress to her life. The church could have loved her and practiced Paul's admonition in Galatians

6:1–2: "Brothers, if someone is caught in a sin, you who are spiritual should restore him gently. But watch yourself, or you also may be tempted. Carry each other's burdens, and in this way you will fulfill the law of Christ." Instead of throwing Denise to the dogs, love should have prevailed to help restore her. The word "restore" in this passage was used to describe setting a fracture or sewing a torn fishing net. Paul stresses the idea of helping the person to be whole again. Shouldn't that be our goal in restoration?

Suggested Approaches

What Denise did was wrong. Her actions were the result of self-deception. But the church didn't need to throw Denise into the court system. In love they could have kept her on as church secretary and helped her financially through a financial counselor. If her problem was budgeting, the counselor could have helped her; if it was too little pay, the church could have reconsidered her hourly rate. By keeping her in the church, they could hold her accountable and love her in the process.

One suggestion for repayment might have been asking her to work one day for free each week until the money was paid back or deducting a certain amount from her weekly check. I would also have given Denise incentives. If over a period of time she continued to be obedient and worked through her problems, grace could have been shown by eliminating a certain amount of the money owed. Denise needed to be loved, more than anything. The example of love the church showed would have been seen by her children and eventually would have made a difference in their views of God.

If for some it was out of the question to keep Denise on as an employee of the church, they could have worked with her to find another job, continued practicing love with her. The church could have connected her with a spiritual mothering group that would affirm her and accept her. I am sure as a result of her experiences she would have had much to offer to the body of Christ. Finally, people like Denise need to be nurtured, listened to, and loved. The church needs to reach out to them instead of throwing them out and pretending the problem never existed.

Conclusion

For some there is no easy way to handle a situation like the one with Denise. Her actions could be the actions of many in the church, given her circumstances. Yet the church did little to stretch out their arms and probe into the pain that motivated her theft. It was easier for the church to press charges and pay a lawyer to handle the case rather than get their hands dirty by helping show love to Denise. Jesus said He came for the sick not for the healthy. What would my response be in a case like this?

What would happen if my board had the same strong interpretation of the truth as in Denise's case but I wanted to show more compassion? How would I appeal to them and what would my reasoning be? In answering these questions we can understand how important it is to understand the different personality types on our boards. Your board, in responding to cases like Denise's or to conflicts in other areas of your ministry, may surprise you, unless you know how God has wired them.

Kurt Bruner writes in his book, *Responsible Living in an Age of Excuses,*

> In order to overcome life's obstacles, we must maintain a balanced perspective of adversity. Yes, life is difficult. But we do not have to remain victims of its downward pull. We can pick up the paddle of responsible living, face the current, and begin actively going against the flow. As someone has said, the difference between stumbling blocks and stepping-stones is the way a man uses them.
>
> Certainly some individuals drift so far downstream that they become overwhelmed by the rapids of adversity. For that reason, it is important that the principles of personal responsibility be applied long before reaching the point of upheaval. Those who fail to do so often place themselves in need of crisis intervention from someone further upstream.[3]

Discussion Questions

- Should the church require restitution? If so, how does this relate to the parable of the unmerciful servant?

- Should the congregation be made aware of Denise's dilemma?

- If discipline is deemed necessary, what type would you administer?

- How can love be shown in this difficult case?

CHAPTER EIGHT

CRISIS PREGNANCIES

DAWN: AN ABORTED DILEMMA

ABORTION IS THE HOT BUTTON of our society, but what do I do when the dilemma of abortion comes to my office? The balance between the present and the future is often blurred by an unexpected teenage pregnancy. The following story doesn't end happily ever after. Instead, it forces us to think what we might say and do when we are thrust into the decision-making process of a teenager and her nonbelieving parents.

At the time, there seemed to be no alternative. It was rush, rush, hurry up.

Dawn is now twenty-five years old. Seven years ago, when she was a senior in high school and had just been awarded a scholarship to a prestigious college, she found out she was pregnant.

Dawn recalls those difficult days. "I met him when a bunch of us went to see a movie. He was sitting behind me and started playing with my long brown hair. At first I was annoyed but after a while I liked the attention. I didn't even concentrate on the movie; I just liked his hands going through my hair. He was a student at our rival high school. Mel and I seemed to have a lot in common. He had high hopes of becoming a dentist and was waiting to hear from a school in the Midwest. He walked me home after the movie and started calling on me regularly. I liked the attention he gave me for who I was and not because of my grades or achievements. He respected me and things never really got out of control sexually until one weekend.

"I told my parents I was going with Mel to visit his grandparents about sixty miles away. During the day a snowstorm came through the area dumping eight inches of blowing snow. I called my folks and they encouraged us to spend the night. No sense risking an accident or getting stuck. His grandparents went to bed upstairs early. We made a fire in their fireplace and he held me for a long time. Things just progressed and before I knew it we were having sex. It wasn't exactly thrilling but neither of us could stop. The next day I didn't ever think I would be pregnant. Six weeks went by before I started to get scared. I wasn't feeling good some mornings and then it hit me. I can't be! What will my folks say? How will Mel respond?

"My mom and I always had a good relationship so I knew I could tell her. She was disappointed and wanted the best for me. But what that meant I wasn't exactly sure of."

It was a crisis in Dawn's family, but none of the family members sought advice or counsel. "We all wanted a quick solution," she recalls. "I think we were all embarrassed." Dawn had been counting on an enjoyable senior year of high school, and her parents had great hopes for her college career.

The emotional pressure of the circumstances built. Dawn's boyfriend broke up with her when she told him about the pregnancy. He refused to be involved. Dawn's parents wanted to avoid a scandal, so they did not press matters with him. Nobody liked the idea of an abortion, but it seemed the best way to get on with normal family life.

Dawn's closest friends were involved in Youth For Christ at their high school and were always talking about their youth pastor. They encouraged her to talk with him. "He will understand," they said. Knowing that her parents were intent on her having an abortion, Dawn made an appointment with Pastor Karl. She told him her dilemma and asked him if there were any other options.

Biblically, Pastor Karl knew abortion was the taking of a child's life and tried to persuade Dawn to have her parents visit a crisis pregnancy center. The conversation did little to change Dawn's mind about her pregnancy. As she went away, a frustrated youth pastor pondered what he would do with the confidential information he had learned. Would he confront her parents or just pray things would work out?

She is just a teenager, he prayed. *What does she know about how this decision might affect her for a long, long time? Lord, give me wisdom. What should I do?*

The abortion took place in the spring of Dawn's senior year. Her parents made sure she was well cared for medically. Afterward, her pregnancy and abortion were never spoken of at home. None of them shared their feelings or even considered other options, but they all pondered different things. The following is a quick synopsis of the consciences of the people involved.

For Dawn's parents, the reputation of their honor-roll daughter and their family pride were at stake. What would their friends say? How widespread would knowledge of her pregnancy become within their social, religious, and occupational spheres? Dawn's parents obviously felt very strongly that the greatest good for their family and for their daughter would be to opt for an abortion. Without taking into consideration the ethical arguments that surround the abortion issue, they considered immediate action to be in the best interest of their daughter's future.

Next is Dawn, who has strong loyalties toward her parents and considered their decision to be best. She is considering a college scholarship that would be uninterrupted if she proceeds with the abortion. On the other hand, Dawn is open to the influence of her friends. She wants to do the right thing.

Pregnancy for some is like catching a cold; you take what you have to and hope it goes away. When confronted with Pastor Karl's option of considering a crisis pregnancy center, her loyalty toward her parents superseded any attempts on Pastor Karl's behalf. In this case, loving the child she has in her womb is secondary to her parents' desires. While the present and the future are clashing in a teenager's life, one can begin to recognize the need for practicing and teaching the importance of biblical ethical decision making as a proactive approach to various situations.

Finally, Pastor Karl is a young man who is thrust into the difficulties of his office. He tries to persuade Dawn to seek help, but since he hasn't developed a relationship of care and respect, this is difficult for him. When she leaves, he has a decision to make if he is passionate about his pro-life convictions. Does he call Dawn's parents and tell the truth about abortion and risk getting in trouble for disclosing confidential information? If so, what would be his approach and persuasive argument?

Here is where loyalties and theology appear to come to an impasse. He only has a certain amount of time to confront Dawn's parents. Doing this will involve a clearly defined ethical strategy that would show concern for Dawn, educate her parents on the trauma of an abortion, and allow her parents to feel that an alternative decision would not necessarily mean a scandalous situation for their family. Does he pray for God to intervene in some way and file the situation in his memory? In taking this approach his conscience would rule more than his theology.

Seven years later, Pastor Karl is a little older and wiser. He is learning the truth does not always appear the same to everyone on issues that seem clearly right and wrong to him.

Decision-Making Tower

For the vast majority of evangelicals, abortion is the taking of a life breathed by God. *Abortion* is a word that creates controversy, anger, hurt, and love. We have witnessed the shouting matches, protests, and media hype surrounding this controversy. You may have marched or blocked the entrances to clinics in your area. Yet there continues to be a suppression of the facts. It is estimated that since *Roe v. Wade* in 1973, over thirty million children have been killed, and we continue to call it contraception. As we process Dawn's case through the Decision-Making Tower, let it make us more aware of those, churched and unchurched, who opt for a quick fix even though their decision lacks any moral justification. Our responsibility is to make our people more conscious of the facts and help put together fragmented emotions after the fact. No one can undo the past, but by God's grace we can allow His love to massage and heal our pain (see fig. 8.1).

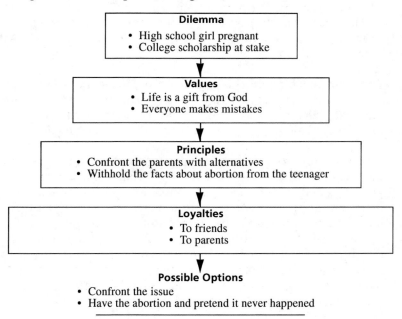

Figure 8.1

Ethical Guidelines

Sometimes the most difficult decisions in the ministry are those that involve people who do not want your help but reveal confidential information. "There was once a time when the decision to have an abortion was so private, so secretive, nobody dared mention it in public. Not only was it illegal, it was considered the most intimate of subjects. It was not uncommon for family members to know nothing (which is still true) and for the medical profession to view [it] with disdain. The whole thing was a private decision, and those who did know usually looked the other way. No longer. It is now big business, impacting three major professions of our world: the political, the legal, and for sure the medical."[1]

The reality of life often brings stress, which we seek to resolve in the most convenient way. The pastor who wrestles with confidential information from people like Dawn is often hard-pressed to risk helping those who do not have the decision-making power to consider other options.

- Develop a network of agencies that will give support to the teenager(s) and parents.[2]
- Teach your high schoolers Josh McDowell's series *Right from Wrong,* in order to teach young people how to make better decisions so they might be prepared to help a friend in this situation.
- Find families who have faced Dawn's dilemma and made wise choices.

The bottom line for pastors is to get involved in the lives of our young people. Our society is aggressively wooing them away from the church through materialism, sensual desires, and the lie that being somebody has more to do with your image than with the person on the inside.

Never before has our society's understanding of sexuality been more in conflict with biblical teaching. Young men and women growing up in our churches are exposed to powerful influences that scorn Scripture's admonitions to purity, the sanctity of the marriage relationships, and the absolute condemnation of homosexuality. These influences occur as examples within the family or among friends, strong approval of promiscuity in contemporary literature, music and television programming, and federally-funded sex education programs from organizations like Planned Parenthood, which are totally amoral in their approach. Sex is presented as an isolated experience of pleasure unrelated to the rest of life. Our children need direction from the Bible.[3]

Our teenagers are crying for help. When we neglect them, stories like Dawn's will continue to echo across the land and even in our sanctuaries.

Biblical Issues

Life is a gift from God. Consider the following passages:

So God created man in his own image, in the image of God he created him; male and female he created them. (Gen. 1:27)

You shall not murder. (Exod. 20:13)

You brought me out of the womb; you made me trust in you even at my mother's breast. From birth I was cast upon you; from my mother's womb you have been my God. (Ps. 22:9–10)

For you created my inmost being; you knit me together in my mother's womb. I praise you because I am fearfully and wonderfully made; your works are wonderful, I know that full well. My frame was not hidden from you when I was made in the secret place. When I was woven together in the depths of the earth, your eyes saw my unformed body. All the days ordained for me were written in your book before one of them came to be. (Ps. 139:13–16)

From Scripture we discover that God created us in His image long before we were ever born. "God set apart Jeremiah from his mother's womb (Jer. 1). He called Isaiah from his mother's womb (Isa. 49), assuming the reference is to the prophet. In the New Testament, the apostle Paul indicates he, too, was set apart by God while in the womb (Gal. 1:15). The Bible gives no suggestion that God regards the unborn as less valuable in his sight than other human beings."[4]

If He is the author and perfecter of life, are Dawn's parents playing God with their daughter and grandchild? Some might say yes, but like so many parents they felt they had few alternatives and little time.

The emotional paralysis that occurs after a parent hears the words, "I think I'm pregnant" numbs him or her to the possibilities. Similar to a political race, the unknown candidate who plasters his name in front of your face is more likely to get your vote. That is the strategy of Planned Parenthood. In considering Scripture we can think of Abraham and Hagar in Genesis 16. God had made a covenant with Abram in Genesis 12:2–3, "I will make you into a great nation and I will bless you; I will make your name great, and you will be a blessing. I will bless those who bless you, and whoever curses you I will curse; and all peoples on earth will be blessed through you." Over time this covenant became confusing to Abram because he was childless.

Sarai, Abram's wife, was frustrated also. So she told Abram to sleep with their maidservant Hagar. In Genesis 16:4–6 Scripture tells us, "When she [Hagar] knew she was pregnant, she began to despise her mistress. Then Sarai said to Abram, 'You are responsible for the wrong I am suffering. I put my servant in your arms, and now that she knows she is pregnant, she despises me. May the LORD judge between you and me.' 'Your servant is in your hands,' Abram said. 'Do with her whatever you think best.' Then Sarai mistreated Hagar; so she fled."

Hagar was in a crisis. Pregnant with Abram's child, she flees the wrath of Sarai. The angel of the Lord found her and ministered to her. Hagar went back and submitted to Sarai, and God blessed her with Ishmael. In her distress, God was near. In the same way He was near to Hagar in her distress, God is still near to those women in similar situations. God has chosen to use His body the church to show compassion and care. For women in a crisis pregnancy with nowhere to turn there are loving people who are there to help. Crisis Pregnancy Centers (CPC), skills classes for unwed mothers, and other such groups are an extension of the hand of God in a difficult situation. Compassion and care are the real issue.

Suggested Approaches

If we want to do something about changing the tide of premarital sex and the potential for abortion then we need to be proactive in our approach. Yes, inevitably there will be situations like Dawn's that catch us off guard. My prayer is that we will prepare ourselves ahead of time for time bombs like this one. I have outlined some suggestions.

First, teach your children the necessity of abstinence not only because Scripture says sex outside of marriage is wrong, but because our young people need to know the decisions they make will last for a lifetime: the mind keeps replaying that one-night stand; mourning the broken relationship, the betrayal of love; reliving the abortion; missing the child given up for adoption. We wish there was a rewind button in our lives so we could edit those times that haunt us. But there isn't!

The pressures on teenagers is incredible. They need our guidance and help. Being a part of the in group can cause a teen to rationalize his or her convictions. As I mentioned before, McDowell's book and video series *Right from Wrong* is an excellent place to start. Let your teens know that being cool isn't accomplished by doing what everyone else does.

Second, support your local Campus Crusade, Youth For Christ, Younglife, or other group that is in your local high school. Pray for them, volunteer to help with their activities, and support them financially if you can. Your involvement, in many instances, will give you the privilege of being on campus, which in many high schools is difficult these days.

Belonging to a group will be a tremendous source of strength and encouragement for teens. I remember, during my high school days in Chicago, everyone in our church youth group bought a jacket with the church's name on the back. We wore those blue jackets everywhere. They not only gave us an identity, but they also created a healthy youth-group image.

Third, and most important, pray, pray, and pray often for the young people of your church. Develop a prayer emphasis for specific families and teens. James wrote that the prayer of a righteous man accomplishes much. For all the kids in his youth group, Jeff Mcqueary, youth pastor at Moody Church, has prayer sponsors—saints who love and care about the teens enough to call upon heaven for their protection, for wisdom, and for God's love to hold them tight. There is a battle raging not only in our schools and on the streets, but in the heavenly places too.

Finally, love those who have had the misfortune of Dawn, an eighteen-year-old who wants to please her parents and who hurts deep inside. Show them that God forgives their sin and loves them like they have never been loved before because of what Jesus did at Calvary. I can't read through Scripture from Genesis to Revelation without finding God's love and forgiveness all over the pages. How he dealt with Matthew, the woman at the well, constantly forgiving the nation of Israel, using Hosea as a symbol of His unchanging love, and many other examples reveal His plan of redemption. Dawn will live with her decision for the rest of her life, but she needs to know the Savior who took her pain when He spread out His arms at Calvary and said, It is paid in full.

Conclusion

One pre-Christmas season a young family spent all day Saturday making homemade candy and cookies. After dinner the kids were told to go and put their pajamas on while mom finished cleaning up the dishes. Startled by a reflection, she glanced at a mirror that provided an unobstructed view into the dining room where the homemade goodies were stored—and where the family parakeet was kept.

She watched intently (careful to bang an occasional pan) while her oldest son, then seven, tiptoed into the dining room, put his blanket over the parakeet's cage, and then summoned his sisters to join him for the "take." They scurried into the dining room and filled their pockets with candy and cookies. Satisfied that their supply would last through the night, the girls headed for the bedroom. Their brother lingered only long enough to take the blanket off the bird's cage.

Within a few minutes their mom came and demanded that they give up the goods. The two girls looked at their brother with an evil eye. He shouted back, "I covered the bird, I swear I covered the bird."[5]

Hebrews 4:13 says, "Nothing in all creation is hidden from God's sight. Everything is uncovered and laid bare before the eyes of him to whom we must give account." We laugh at the little boy, yet we think God doesn't see our lives. He does. Scripture says nothing is hidden from the eyes of God.

When we avoid the harsh realities of teenagers' lives, in a sense we cover the cage. Denying the problem and avoiding the consequences of our actions only complicates the issue later. If you are a parent, don't wait for a crisis before you get involved in your child's life. Pass on a legacy of love that communicates trust, meaningful involvement, and a caring relationship. You will thus lay a good foundation so that the winds of life won't blow your children away.

Discussion Questions

- If you were in Pastor Karl's shoes, how would you have handled the situation?

- Is abortion always wrong?

- How would you minister to the family after the situation?

- What kind of teaching would you give to your young people?

———◆———

BETH: ANGRY CONFESSIONS

THE FOLLOWING STORY ABOUT a pregnant teenager brings to light the issue of confidentiality and the conflict of a double standard. It involves the chaplain of a Bible school, but we can liken this relationship to a multiple-staff church. Are confidential meetings strictly between the pastor and the parishioner? Or are they open for discussion during staff meetings?

Beth was eighteen when she became pregnant. She knew her relationship with Andrew had gotten out of control. They tried double dating and group activities to avoid sexual intimacy. These worked for a while, but even though they were cautious, Beth found herself pregnant.

Andrew and Beth were attending a small Bible college. This environment made things especially difficult. They both knew abortion was out of the question, and Beth had misgivings about adoption.

Beth asked if she could meet with Pastor Sumner, the chaplain at the college. The conversation went something like this:

Pastor Sumner: "Beth, I appreciate your involvement and enthusiasm for Christ. Your presence really makes a difference on campus."

Beth: "Thanks."

Pastor Sumner: "What is on your mind?"

Beth: "Well . . . [a pause as tears begin to form and roll down her cheek]. This is really hard for me to talk about. If I tell you something, will you promise not to tell anyone else?"

Pastor Sumner: "Beth, you can trust me. I will have your best interests in mind."

Beth: "For about a year now . . ."

Beth spends the next hour telling Pastor Sumner about her relationship with Andrew and hesitantly informs him she is pregnant.

At the founding of the school the president of the college had made a ruling that disciplinary action would be taken if any female students became pregnant. They would be expelled from school. Beth knew the only way she could remain on campus was to marry Andrew.

Beth became angry about the double standard. Andrew did not face expulsion.

Several weeks went by, and Beth was called into the president's office.

"I understand you are pregnant," said President Mayer.

Beth remained quiet; her mind raced ahead to the disappointment and humiliation her parents would feel. Little did she know the worst was yet to come.

"You know the rules, Beth," President Mayer barked at her. "Not only am I upset, but I want you to know you have blemished the reputation of this fine institution. I am not only going to expel you from school, but I demand that you confess your sin to the entire student body in chapel tomorrow."

Beth was angered and stunned. *How could he do this to me. How would he feel if I were his daughter? What about Andrew? If this is what it means to model Christ's love I will be glad to leave here!*

Forced to leave her education because of the pregnancy, Beth became disillusioned with Christianity. Bitterness entered her relationship with her parents, and she immediately stopped attending church.

At the insistence of her parents, Beth began counseling to gain insight into her feelings of anger and bitterness.

Decision-Making Tower

As chaplain of the college, what was Pastor Sumner's responsibility to Beth? Instead of setting up an appointment to further discuss the situation and work toward a good solution, he quickly deferred the situation to the college president. Pastor Sumner's idea of trust was not what Beth was expecting. Had she known the outcome, I wonder if she would have withheld the information and sought out other help. Our analysis gives us a clear picture of two options. If you hold strongly to the saying, "rules are rules," then Beth gets what she deserves. In fact, she is evidence of a common biblical truth, you reap what you sow. On the other hand, if you have a strong personality and love ethic, then you will seek the best possible solution for Beth.

Teen pregnancy is exempt from geographical location. Urban or rural, the situation remains the same. How will we handle it (see fig. 8.2)?

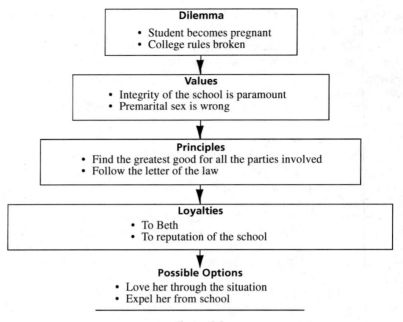

Figure 8.2

Ethical Guidelines

"Counseling involves helping people make decisions. Pregnancy is a marker in people's lives. It is one of the most visible signs of transition from one stage of life to another. During that stage, numerous decisions are made. Some people decide between abortion and keeping the child. Others decide between raising the child and giving it up for adoption. Most decide how to conduct their lives after the birth of the child. The community must decide how it will react to the people."[6]

This case reflects Chaplain Sumner's inability to work out a moral and biblical decision. Teenage pregnancy isn't just something you can dismiss. Feelings of guilt as well as the joy of carrying a new life confuse the issue. A teen's own emotions fused with the reactions of a boyfriend, parents, and in this case the school president, all converge. How would the situation have changed if it had been Sumner's daughter? or the president's daughter? We must recognize we are dealing with whole families and not just the pregnant teenager.

"When a pregnant adolescent decides to include you in her decision making and in her efforts to cope with her problem pregnancy, she is usually not merely asking for information about which decisions to make and how to make those decisions. She also wants your support and acceptance."[7]

In spite of your reaction she needs to know you love her and care about her. This may be difficult because of the strong personal values you live by. That is why it is so important to have a framework to process these sensitive issues through. The temptation is to transfer our values into a judgmental or condemning attitude toward the hurting teen. Here are some guidelines you can practice before a crisis occurs:

- As parents we need to continue to teach our children values.
- Instead of letting our teens learn about sex on the school playground or from inappropriate movies, plan a special elective for fathers and sons, mothers and daughters taught by a Christian counselor. In so doing teens will have a better understanding of sex from a biblical perspective and gain the strength to say no.
- Work to maintain an open line of communication with your kids.

The influence of our ethical decisions regarding teenage pregnancies impacts families as well. The responsibility given to ministers in this area is critical. We must carefully consider the result of our ethical decisions. Beth's case is probably more common than realized. An article in *Fortune* magazine titled, "The New Wave of Illegitimacy" revealed the following statistics: "More than one million of the U.S.'s nine million girls between the ages of 15 and 19 get pregnant every year. Roughly half give birth; the rest either miscarry or have abortions. These pregnancies happen despite the fact that 93% of the nation's high schools teach sex education."[8]

Biblical Issues

Paul says in 1 Thessalonians that God's will for us is to flee sexual immorality. It is a clear warning against those who desire sexual activity. In Proverbs, Solomon continues to write on the theme of wisdom so as not to be tempted in this area. Beth's actions were clearly disobedient to the Word and the college rules. Wasn't her punishment considered fair for someone who was sexually active at a Christian college?

She also knows what the Bible says about premarital sex. Couldn't we say that Beth's blatant display could be used as a deterrent for other couples who have had the desire to go too far? In fact, Beth's situation could be meant for the good of the whole school. The truth as well as prescribed codes should be enforced. When we weave this type of decision making into our understanding of Scripture we become like the Pharisees in Jesus' day. Beth's actions are heartbreaking for any parent and school official. But this is not the place for inflexible decision making. When we take this approach we eventually worsen rather than improve an already bad situation. When we choose to deny or to please those around us we lose the perspective that Jesus had for people.

But Beth's situation could be considered from another biblical view. What about the pastor's and the president's responsibility to Beth as a sister in Christ? We can assume they are her parents' age. As those who are leaders and well-seasoned in the Word, could they have been more compassionate instead of judicial? John 8:3–11 says,

> The teachers of the law and the Pharisees brought in a woman caught in adultery. They made her stand before the group and said to Jesus, "Teacher, this woman was caught in the act of adultery. In the Law Moses commanded us to stone such women. Now what do you say?" They were using this question as a trap, to have a basis for accusing him.
>
> But Jesus bent down and started to write on the ground with his finger. When they kept on questioning him, he straightened up and said to them, "If any one of you is without sin, let him be the first to throw a stone at her." Again he stooped down and wrote on the ground.
>
> At this, those who heard began to go away one at a time, the older ones first, until only Jesus was left, with the woman still standing there. Jesus straightened up and asked her, "Woman, where are they? Has no one condemned you?"
>
> "No one, sir," she said.
>
> "Then neither do I condemn you," Jesus declared. "Go now and leave your life of sin."

The Master's approach was to show grace because He knows our hearts. The issue comes down to love. The sin, guilt, and humiliation of the teenagers will be brought to light by the convicting power of the Holy Spirit. "Let me then establish a principle. Sexual sin calls for repentance from the sinner and forgiveness from God. In addition it calls for compassionate understanding and help from Christians, especially where complex psychological factors are associated with it."[9]

The biblical issue becomes a weaving of love and help, searching for the best possible solution for all parties involved. You won't need to remind Beth of her sin. When her child is born, a whole new set of dynamics will emerge.

Suggested Approaches

How can we help out Beth? It is very important that we communicate trust and acceptance to the teenager, as hard as that may be. Yes, you may become disappointed in her. I know in my experience in the ministry I have. Assure her that you will be her advocate as you get her parents and other key people in the church involved. Seek Mill's principle of finding the greatest good. This is not only a crisis for the teenager, but embarrassing for the parents, especially if they are leaders in the church. The love that God shows through us will be modeled and remembered for a long time. Or, you may lose a church family because of the way you misrepresent God's love.

If you have extreme difficulty or are fresh in the ministry and wonder how to handle this type of crisis, seek out a mentor. A wiser, more seasoned pastor can give you guidance. Or find a couple who has experienced this pain and draw upon their experience. Learn how they felt, what they did right, and what they did wrong.

Conclusion

"The girl's immediate need for advice and acceptance does not eliminate her need for forgiveness and absolution. Yet forgiveness follows confession and repentance. Confession is brought about in the most effective senses by the work of the Holy Spirit. Our initial job is not to be the hammer of the Holy Spirit through guilt manipulation. We are to be the vessel of the Holy Spirit for love and acceptance. We might gently raise spiritual and forgiveness issues when appropriate, but generally our most productive role is to be there when the girl is ready to confess her sins, repent, and turn from them."[10]

Our role is not only to minister to her but to get the family involved. Find support for them in order that the body of Christ may function. Every teenage pregnancy is different in the same way every family dynamic is different. There will be times when you will feel overwhelmed and will need to pray harder than other times in your ministry. Make sure you seek God's solution.

Discussion Questions

- Where would you draw the line between following the rules and showing compassion?

- Was it right or necessary that Chaplain Sumner discuss this with the president? Why or why not?

- Discuss and develop a strategy you might follow if one of your teens confided in you about a pregnancy.

- If you have already experienced this dilemma, how did you handle it? Would you handle it the same way again?

CHAPTER NINE

WHEN THE CLOSET IS OPENED

AN AWFUL AWAKENING

AS PASTORS, WE ARE THRUST into what some might consider the most awkward situations. I am sure your ministry experience will affirm this. In the following story we will see how one pastor deals with the delicate issue of homosexuality when a church member's son admits to his gay lifestyle.

Pastor Carl Wasser awoke with a start. It felt like the ringing phone had lodged somewhere in his spine. Carl half shuffled, half dashed to the kitchen. The clock glowing on the microwave told him it was 2:37 A.M. "Hello?"

"Oh, I'm so glad you're there!" The voice was male and it sounded tense. Commotion filled the background. "I'm really sorry for getting you up like this, but I need your help. I'm in jail."

The circuits in Carl's mind had warmed up by now. "May I ask who this is?"

"Oh, I'm sorry. This is Ted Klein, you know, Art and Edna's son." Of course Carl knew him. His parents were deeply involved in Meadowwood Community Church, and Teddy—that is what everyone called him—had grown up in the church. Now he was in college across town.

"You're in jail? What kind of trouble are you in?"

"Look, I need you to come bail me out." Ted avoided answering the question. "I can give you the money tomorrow, but I need to get out of this place tonight. I get only one call, so I called you. Can you help me? I know it's a lot to ask."

"Are your mom and dad out of town? Why didn't you call them?" Carl could dodge questions, too.

"Hey, I couldn't do that! No way. They would just die. I turned to you because you're my minister and I need help. Can't you just come get me?"

"Ted, what are you in for? Why can't you tell your parents?"

"I'd rather not say over the phone. Look, won't you please come help me?"

Carl wasn't without a heart. "Okay, Ted. It'll be about thirty minutes. How much is your bail?"

"Better bring a couple hundred bucks."

"I'm on my way. But one thing. When I get there, I'm going to expect some straight answers."

All the way downtown, Carl wondered if he were doing the right thing. *Should I have called Art? Why won't the kid say what the matter is? What kind of fool am I to be traipsing downtown at this hour of the night? What is Teddy up to anyway? What can I do to help him?*

He pulled into the parking lot and found the jail entrance. From the open windows above, gruff voices and cursing filtered through the iron mesh. *I can see why he doesn't want to spend the night,* Carl thought as he blinked in the bright light of the doorway.

"I am here to see Theodore Klein," Carl told the desk sergeant. "I believe he was arrested earlier this evening."

The sergeant straightened up and squinted at Carl. "You his father?" It wasn't a particularly nasty look, but it was not friendly, either.

"No, I'm not. I'm his pastor."

"Pastor!" Now he looked genuinely amused. "You know what we picked him up for? We caught that little dirtbag parked by the city pool with two prostitutes—male prostitutes!" The sergeant paused to see what kind of response that would raise.

Carl's face blanched, but he retained his composure. "Can I bail him out?"

"Yeah. We'll be glad to get rid of him. That will be two hundred bucks, and he will have to promise to appear for a preliminary hearing in the morning." Carl handed over the money, collected one grateful and scared kid, and drove toward the college.

The car was filled with awkward silence. Finally Carl spoke. "The officer told me why you were arrested. You know you're going to have to tell your parents."

"I know," Ted replied, hanging his head. "Would you help me? I don't even know where to begin."

"You will have to do the talking, but, yes, I'll stay with you while you do it. Just tell them the truth."

When they got to the college, Ted reluctantly made the call. His parents were stunned.

After Ted told them the bare bones, Carl spoke reassuringly to them.

"Ted's okay. He's got a hearing at 9 A.M. Yes, I'll attend with you." At 4:30 Carl finally crawled back into bed.

The next few days Carl spoke frequently with Ted and his parents. He walked them through the hearing the next day. Ted did not get any jail time, but he was pretty shaken by the severity of the legal process. He realized he was in real trouble.

Ted was lucky in one sense. News of his brush with the law did not hit the papers. As far as Carl knew, only Ted and his parents were aware of Ted's problem. And none of them were about to let the church know.

Before long, Ted moved his things out of his parents' home. He moved in with a single guy from church. Jeremy, his roommate, was straight. He just needed someone to share the rent. Carl wondered, *Should I tell Jeremy about Ted? He ought to know, I suppose, but I can't break confidence with Ted.* Carl said nothing.

Later, Ted began dating a girl from church. Carl viewed this as a pretty good sign, although with mixed emotions. After they had dated pretty steadily for a number of weeks, the young woman made an appointment with Carl.

"Pastor," she said, sitting on the couch across from his chair, "you know Ted and I have been dating. I like Ted, and I'm not sure this is a problem, but my friend encouraged me to talk to you. I'm not sure exactly how to say this, but Ted has . . . has difficulty expressing any affection. Is he gay?"

Carl swallowed hard. "Cindy, that is something you are going to have to ask him. Think about it for a minute. If Ted were gay and I knew it, should I tell you?"

Cindy asked Ted, and to his credit, he told her the truth. They struggled through a few more weeks of dating, but it was too big a hurdle for her to get over.

By this point many in Meadowwood Church were catching on. Most felt concern more than condemnation.[1]

Decision-Making Tower

Our personal bias may be strong as we deal with the issue of homosexuality. "As more and more issues surface, the need for biblical and moral options becomes greater. One of the advantages of a framework based, at least initially, on modes of believing and knowing, rather than on beliefs per se, is that it underscores how bias and subjectivity necessarily creep into any discussion of values, even when an attempt is made to keep the discussion as fair and objective as possible."[2] Depending on your convictions concerning the homosexual lifestyle, a roundtable discussion could produce arguments for either concern or condemnation (see fig. 9.1).

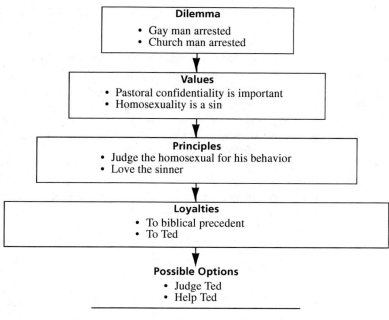

Figure 9.1

Ethical Guidelines

As the gay lifestyle becomes more open, those in the church who have practiced or wrestle with homosexuality will become more common. Guy Charles gives these eight guidelines for effectively ministering to the homosexual:

1. Listen with an open mind to the homosexual who attempts to unburden his or her problem, regardless of the language or descriptions used.
2. Always remember that the homosexual is redeemable from his or her sexual lifestyle. If it was possible in the early church, it is possible now. The only requisite is a desire to change on the part of the individual.
3. You can build that desire within the individual by showing the love of Jesus Christ rather than the condemnation of man. In the face of such love, the individual will judge his or her lifestyle and find it lacking.
4. Do not quote Scripture that condemns the sin unless you're asked to name them. Rather, quote passages that proclaim deliverance from sin and promises of life and hope.

5. After a counseling relationship of trust has been established, get the individual to make a new commitment to Jesus Christ as his or her personal Savior.

6. Although the sexual desire for a homosexual lifestyle may be taken away immediately upon confession of guilt before God, this is not always the case. Remember that the individual is a spiritual child and must be helped to grow in the Christian walk. It may take a day, a week, a month, a year, or even two for a complete liberation from the lifestyle. You must continually be on hand for helpful counseling if the individual falls into old patterns.

7. Make sure that the individual forms Christian relationships within the church community and also that Bible study is included.

8. Remember, you are not accomplishing the miracle of liberation from the lifestyle; neither is the individual the means for his or her own liberation, other than through the desire to change. The Spirit of the living God begins the miracle in the spirit of the individual and defeats the desires of the senses, the flesh, and the sexual appetite through Jesus Christ.[3]

I would like to add several other guidelines that come to mind. Wherever you pastor, become familiar with ministries in your area that minister to former gays and those Christians who are wrestling with the gay lifestyle, and continue to become more educated in the facts of what drives the homosexual.

If you are looking for more information, consider one of the more prominent ministries in North America. Exodus has branch ministries all over the continent. They will direct you to one of their ministries or help you find a referral.

> Exodus International NA
> P.O. Box 77652
> Seattle, WA 98177-0652
> 1-206-784-7799

Biblical Issues

Is homosexuality just another sin? How does the Bible view homosexuality? We read in Genesis 19 that God judged Sodom and Gomorrah by destroying it. One of the reasons for His judgment was the wickedness of the people. Homosexuality was one of their sins. Other mentions of homosexuality are found in Leviticus 18:22: "Do not lie with a man as one lies with a woman; that is detestable." Leviticus 20:13 says, "If a man lies with a man as one lies with a woman, both of them have done what is detestable. They must be put to death; their blood will be on their own heads." Judges 19:22 tells us, "While they were enjoying themselves, some of the wicked men of the city surrounded the house. Pounding on the door, they shouted to the old man who owned the house, 'Bring out the man who came to your house so we can have sex with him.'" Romans 1:25–27 says, "They exchanged the truth of God for a lie, and worshiped and served created things rather than the Creator—who is forever praised. Amen. Because of this, God gave them over to shameful lusts. Even their women exchanged natural relations for unnatural ones. In the same way the men also abandoned natural relations with women and were inflamed with lust for one another. Men committed indecent acts with other men, and received in themselves the due penalty for their perversion."

Finally, 1 Timothy 1:9–10 describes homosexuality as being characteristic of ungodliness. These passages show that homosexuality is unnatural and deserving of God's punishment. However, we must also be careful of "proof texting" the passages in dealing with the issue. Homosexuality is an issue, but we must remember every issue has a person's name attached to it. The Old Testament passages give us insight into Israel's dilemmas and fear of homosexuality even in its day. The passages say the judgment should be death. If we take the punishment of homosexuality literally then we need to use Old Testament law as a literal guide for all of our moral lives.

We need a change in our thinking—not that we lessen our view of sin but that we recognize and remember Jesus died for sinners like you and me—even those who wrestle with homosexuality. "Homosexuality is not the worst sin. It is possibly no worse than any other sin. But it is sin, and God hates all sin and ultimately judges all sin. Like any other sin, however, it is forgivable. And homosexuals are people. I had forgotten that. They are people with a problem. People who are made in the image of God. People who have eternal souls. People who have fallen into the snare of sin. People who are worthy of our time and attention. People whom God loves. People for whom Jesus died. People who will populate heaven because of the love and forgiveness of God."[4]

Suggested Approaches

The issue for Pastor Carl seemed to be clear throughout his dealings with Ted. Let us look at how consistent Pastor Carl was in keeping Ted's problem with homosexuality confidential while lovingly ministering to him.

First, after confronting Ted about the reason for his arrest, Pastor Carl boldly told Ted he must tell his parents the truth. In so doing, Pastor Carl displayed a truth-telling framework and at the same time let Ted break the news to his parents. As difficult and awkward as this may be, the road to healing begins with the truth. His parents needed to know the lifestyle their son was living. Knowing will give them the ability to pray for him and assist him with good counsel.

What would have happened if Pastor Carl had gotten Ted out of his predicament and the next day not told his parents? Like other sexual sins, Ted is not an island in this story. Homosexuals are not born. Since studies have shown that abuse, unbalanced homes, or other dynamics created an abnormal drive and habit, how strained do you think the relationship between Ted and his parents might have been? Instead, with clear reasoning Pastor Carl chose to come alongside Ted as he told his parents the truth. His style was not condemning but courageous in supporting the young man without compromising his position or biblical beliefs. This type of ethical decision making shows us the strength of what Jesus modeled when He walked the earth.

Second, not knowing how long and to what extent Ted was involved in the gay lifestyle, Pastor Carl still felt compelled to maintain his confidence with Ted even if it might have meant a health risk for Jeremy, his roommate. One might suggest that the greatest good for all involved would be for Jeremy to know of Ted's lifestyle. For some in the ministry this would appeal as an appropriate option since it might encourage accountability for Ted.

Finally, Pastor Carl comes to his greatest challenge in maintaining confidentiality. There are many Cindys in the church who feel they should have information about others because of their involvement or genuine concern. Again, Pastor Carl responds to Cindy in a way that maintains his personal integrity as a minister and gives her the option to find out on her own. Who do you tell? When do you tell it? To what extent do you give the facts?

In many cities homosexuality is an openly practiced lifestyle. When a member of your congregation reveals his or her sexual orientation, how will you choose to handle that confidence? Will your response be one of judgment or one of compassion?

Conclusion

Scripture clearly condemns homosexuality as a sin. But like other types of sexual sins, there is hope through God's transforming grace for those who wrestle with sexuality. The measure of God's love must be our underlying standard. The same standard by which we make judgments on the homosexual we should apply to heterosexual behavior outside of marriage.

"The Christian directed by God's Word must avoid both an unholy sympathy for the homosexual and an unholy hatred for the homosexual. . . . It may be easier to take an extreme attitude either of self-righteous hostility or of unrighteous sympathy, but neither extreme is pleasing to our Lord. To please him our attitude must reflect His—in all His purity and grace."[5]

Discussion Questions

- Can a person be a Christian homosexual?

- Search the Scriptures and find verses that will give hope to those who need to hear God's promises.

- What ways can your church minister to the homosexual community?

- If Ted's situation were published in the local newspaper, what would you do with the information if your congregation wanted more facts?

SAYING TOO MUCH IN A PRAYER MEETING

THE FOLLOWING IS A different situation that involves a person's past lifestyle, confidentiality, and the freedom some might feel to share another's personal business during the church's prayer time.

I first met Randy in a Bible study I led in a downtown office building. After the study, we would walk back toward Michigan Avenue to catch a bus or walk to our destinations.

About once a month we would have lunch at the Corner Cafe. Randy wanted me to know he was well-versed in Scripture. I sensed something was different. At the beginning of our study in the book of Amos, he brought a commentary and began explaining the meaning of several of the Hebrew words.

Randy had attended New Life Church for about ten years. He was a committed choir member and was actively involved in the small-group ministry.

One particular lunch together, Randy began to tell me his background. He had two older brothers, both married, and he had graduated from a Christian college with a degree in psychology. After college he attended a very prominent seminary. He never finished because of lack of funds.

I listened with discernment, waiting for the "punch line." I thought, *Why is he telling me all this?* I soon found out. After the long introduction Randy began to tell me about his struggle with homosexuality.

"I had difficulty dating and desired companionship. When I landed this present job ten years ago, I moved away from my parents and found a roommate. Christianity didn't mean much to me at the time because I was making big money."

About two months into a yearlong lease, Randy realized his roommate was gay.

"I did not condemn it because I thought I had an open mind, even though I knew it was wrong. Soon I began to go with my roommate to some of his parties and really had a good time. I guess my need for friendship in a big city caught me off guard," Randy said.

As time went on Randy soon became emotionally involved and eventually sexually active in the gay community.

"I limited myself to one partner at a time, just like a heterosexual male," he said.

For seven years Randy lived the gay lifestyle. Then one winter he caught a cold and could not shake it. After going to the doctor, Randy learned he was HIV positive.

Randy commented, "That is where I am today. The AIDS is very active in my body, and I have to constantly watch myself."

Our lunch ended, and as I left the restaurant I thought, *Who would have ever known? I guess you can't judge a book by its cover.*

I did not mention Randy's situation to anyone and continued my ministry responsibilities.

About two months later, on a Wednesday night during the prayer time as my head was bowed, I listened as the associate pastor prayed.

"Lord, thank you for your love for us. This evening we pray for our brother Randy who has wrestled with homosexuality and has AIDS."

My mouth dropped wide open as my head raised up and my eyes opened wide. *Who does he think he is! What is he trying to prove? How will Randy feel about all of us after this stunt?*

The prayer meeting ended and I watched as Randy got up and walked out.

Decision-Making Tower

When confidentiality is broken in the context of spirituality, a breakdown occurs in our relationship with the congregation. The most humiliating situation a church member can experience is when his or her private life is hung on the line for all to see. Sometimes this is done in the same manner the Pharisees proclaimed their so-called superior righteousness. Professional ethics must be practiced by pastors who shepherd the flock.

The nature of the ministry places us in situations where we are the ones listening to the deepest secrets, darkest pains, and greatest joys of our people. I know there are times when I wonder, *Lord, how much more can a person endure in one lifetime!* The evidence of sin is hidden in the minds of people, but some sins reveal themselves through disease, emotional breakdowns, personality disorders, and in other ways. The question remains, what are we to do with all this information? Our analysis clearly displays how differently two staff members viewed the information they heard. The one chose to follow Kant's truth-telling principle, thinking the body might share in Randy's trouble, while the other pastor chose to remain silent, protecting the confidential trust he had established with Randy (see fig. 9.2).

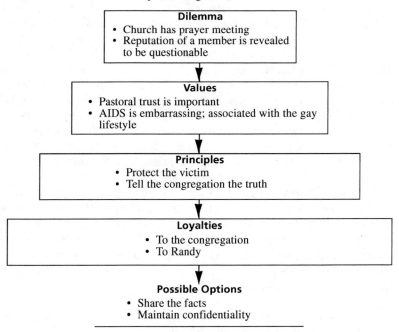

Dilemma
- Church has prayer meeting
- Reputation of a member is revealed to be questionable

Values
- Pastoral trust is important
- AIDS is embarrassing; associated with the gay lifestyle

Principles
- Protect the victim
- Tell the congregation the truth

Loyalties
- To the congregation
- To Randy

Possible Options
- Share the facts
- Maintain confidentiality

Figure 9.2

Ethical Guidelines

This case will help us think through what some guidelines are for sharing private information. For example, what about the pastor who stands in front of his congregation and announces that there are five new pregnant women in their church. Is even this a breach of confidentiality? But in all honesty there are six pregnant women—the sixth one is his wife but he has chosen to withhold that information from the congregation at this time!

"Confidentiality raises several interesting and important ethical issues, in particular over the limits of confidentiality, and the purpose of it. Given that one is told a matter in confidence, is one ever bound to disclose it? A confidential relationship is a special case of promisemaking, and the same general considerations apply."[6]

"A prayer request can break a confidence. It can demonstrate I am knowledgeable about sensational situations, but in the long run, sharing such information can damage our credibility."[7]

Randy could hardly be called someone known by all. In fact, he is more often quiet, keeping to himself, living the reality of his past lifestyle. The associate pastor who thought a prayer meeting voided any level of confidentiality consciously felt right is right and wrong is wrong. To him, Randy's condition was the result of a sinful lifestyle. In praying for Randy, the associate pastor revealed an insensitivity to Randy's situation.

There are times when we lightly take what our people have said and use it as fodder at our next staff meeting. How many times have we gone into these meetings ready to tell the "you will never believe this one" story. People entrust us with their pains, their heartaches, in order that we can pray more effectively and minister to them in a special way. These are our sheep that David talks about in Psalm 23, the ones who need ointment applied or who are thirsty and need extra care. I am not saying it is wrong as a staff to discuss the pain of our people, but do so in a manner of respect, for they too have been made in the image of God. In the same way, at ministerial meetings sharing your heart about someone should be done knowing we are professionals who are called by God to feed His people. Jesus, speaking to Peter asked him, "Do you love me? . . . Feed my sheep." This is our calling. So when can we share this information and seek counsel from others? "Ethical thinking requires reflection and analysis. Lacking that, an individual may assume a mantle of righteousness when one is, in fact, a prisoner of events."[8] Here are some things to think over.

- Discuss as a staff/ministerial group some confidentiality guidelines concerning the information shared in meetings.
- When dealing with people, ask if they want this issue to remain confidential and then discuss what that means to you.
- Let it be known at staff meetings or at ministerial meetings your discussion is to seek the counsel of those present, not to gossip.

By following these guidelines, your personal integrity will continue to grow. The issue of confidentiality boils down to a matter of trust. If our people know they can trust us, the relationship we will have with them will be more meaningful. "One important justification of confidentiality is to preserve human integrity, and to allow the formation of close human bonds."[9]

Biblical Issues

The story in Genesis 37 concerning Joseph raises some issues as we think of confidentiality. You know the story: Joseph had some dreams and told his brothers about them and what they meant. The interpretation of them infuriated his brothers. His brothers were jealous of their father's favorite, the dream maker. So while they were in the fields they plotted to kill him. But Reuben, probably motivated by guilt, tried to rescue Joseph from death at his brothers' hands. So instead they stripped Joseph of his robe, threw him in a cistern, and eventually sold him to some Midianite merchants. Their scheme led them to slaughter a goat and dip the robe in the blood. Each silently trusted the confidentiality of the other brothers. They lived in fear their sin would find them out. For years none of them betrayed the confidence of the others. They had sinned. Their root of jealousy gave birth to the pain in Jacob's heart. Yet they trusted each other. They told no one.

From the wrong motivation for keeping a confidence, we find Joseph's brothers maintaining their vow of silence. Why do we find it much easier to keep silent for the wrong reasons than to maintain confidence on real issues? What about the pastor who stays in a hotel out of town for a conference. On several nights he and a pastor friend watch inappropriate movies. Who would think of blowing the whistle? Or how about the pastor who shares with his friend some of the ways he bypassed paying the IRS last year. Can we justify keeping a confidence if truth telling will create a messy situation? We all feel important if we can share some tidbits that others don't know yet. "Have you heard about so-and-so?"

Proverbs 20:19 says, "A gossip betrays a confidence; so avoid a man who talks too much." There is little specific teaching in Scripture about confidentiality. In Luke 2 when the Jews went to Jerusalem for the Feast of Passover, Jesus stayed behind to teach in the temple. Upon his return Mary said to him, "Your father and I have been anxiously searching for you." Jesus replied, "Why were you searching for me? Didn't you know I had to be in my Father's house?" They didn't understand his statement. The text goes on to say, "Mary treasured all these things in her heart." She kept them to herself. Our position needs to be on our knees when our people share their deepest struggles. I believe this is one reason why psychotherapy has become so common in our generation. We are so busy building the church that we have neglected to genuinely care for its people. Christian therapists offer a safe and secure place for those who are hurting to bring their burdens and feel like they are being cared for. Let us be careful with the information given to us.

Jesus called Matthew, the tax collector, to come and follow Him. We read in Matthew 9:10–13:

> While Jesus was having dinner at Matthew's house, many tax collectors and "sinners" came and ate with him and his disciples. When the Pharisees saw this, they asked his disciples, "Why does your teacher eat with tax collectors and 'sinners'?"
>
> On hearing this, Jesus said, "It is not the healthy who need a doctor, but the sick. But go and learn what this means: 'I desire mercy, not sacrifice.' For I have not come to call the righteous, but sinners."

Instead of talking, let's do more praying. As we listen let's continue to seek ways the church can minister to those who hurt. No matter what is said and kept behind closed doors, nothing is kept secret from God.

Suggested Approaches

One approach to this delicate situation is to have another meeting with Randy. Ask him how he is doing. Discuss with him the extent of his illness and ask him who he has told and suggest the possibility of sharing it with the church in smaller settings. Depending on the size of the church, word will get around quickly. Keep in mind that the love of God needs to prevail. The consequences of Randy's lifestyle are literally killing him. He does not need the church to judge him at this time. Instead, be supportive and a source of encouragement. Telling the truth in a prayer meeting may seem appropriate, but only at the right time.

Since the associate pastor shared this confidential issue with the congregation, someone needs to bring him and Randy together to talk about it. In order for the body of Christ to be built up, good communication is necessary. Bringing the two of them together will help heal Randy's feelings and give him insight on how the associate pastor approaches ministry.

Conclusion

The issue of confidentiality raises some other issues. How can the church continue to minister more effectively to its people? No matter what the size of your church, begin or continue to develop a small-group ministry. People like Randy need a core group of others who will continue to pray for him, help him, and befriend him.

I remember a man at Moody Church named Jim who was in the last stages of AIDS, which he had contracted because of bad choices earlier in his life. He was connected to several small groups and was a part of the church choir. As he progressively worsened, different people brought him food, visited him, and cared for him. Those who loved him as a brother in Christ showed mercy and put their words into action. After Jim died, he was remembered for his love for God and involvement with those in the choir and his small groups. The people who ministered to him felt better because they were used by God to help the people Jesus talked about.

Discussion Questions

- Is it okay to share with our wives the things we have heard in confidence?

- What issues are we bound by law to disclose?

- Now that others know about Randy, should the whole church know?

- What ministry can your church begin or further develop to minister to those who are hurting?

CHAPTER TEN

CONCLUDING THOUGHTS

I NEVER IN MY wildest dreams anticipated the types of situations people get themselves into. My telephone rings and in the back of my mind I still wonder, *What now?* Only now I am a few years older and have more wisdom in my backpack. I seek the counsel of others because I have come to understand my limitations and as a result am more secure with how God has made me. Much of my experience began with this phone call.

"Hello, Pastor, this is Tim."

"Hi Tim. How are you?" I replied.

"Not very good," he said. "Pastor, I'm at Pam's house. She has been acting strange lately, and I suspected something was wrong. Pastor, I was right. She told me she thinks she might be pregnant."

"Oh, Tim," I said disappointedly.

"No, Pastor, not me but her stepfather. He's been sexually abusing her."

Several seconds passed and then Tim said, "I called the juvenile officer and she is on her way here now. I wanted to call you, too."

"Thanks Tim," I said.

Several hours later the phone rang again. It was Pam's mother. "Pastor, Pam is at the police station. What kind of trouble is she in?" she asked.

I picked up Pam's parents and drove them to the police station. I sat with Pam's mom as police took her husband away for questioning. Time passed like a cold winter day in Montana as we waited in that little room. The conversation was brief as my thoughts drifted in and out.

How is Pam feeling? What will I say to her stepfather? What will happen to this family? How will this affect the church?

Finally, the juvenile officer entered the room and told us that Pam's stepdad had confessed to abusing her sexually. Her mother's world crumbled to pieces.

"Not that!" she cried. "It can't be true! Anything but that!" I sat there numb.

I thought of Pam. Her innocence was gone. Her life was scarred. She was deceived by someone she trusted and loved. If only this were a nightmare so she might wake up to find it not true. Right now her life seemed shattered. She would have to make sense out of everything and put her life back together. I could not help but think how she would secretly rerun her life again and again every time she entered a trusting relationship.

Since the events of that fall night, I have learned much about myself as a pastor in relationship to others. Since those early years of ministry, I have learned the importance of regularly evaluating my life and my ministry. I cannot emphasize that enough. Taking a periodic inventory of my spiritual, psychological, emotional, and physical well-being helps maintain a balanced life and ministry.

As a result of my experience, I am becoming a student of myself. When I stop doing this, I begin deceiving myself. This is especially significant in light of the many who have stumbled as they have run the race.

As I reflect on my experiences, I see how I went through three phases early in ministry: the idealized pastorate, the actualized experience, and the synthesizing process. I learned much from negative personal experiences that resulted from bad decisions and the inability to cope with certain personality types I encountered during my ministry. The feelings of failure, loss, and the triumph of discovery all came together as God worked in my life. Here is my journey.

In 1980, I began study for a Master of Divinity at Trinity Evangelical Divinity School. I prided myself for going to one of the best seminaries in the country. I sat under the professors who wrote major works in the evangelical community.

At that time, I had no real concept of what pastoral ministry would be like. My only role models were the handful of pastors I knew while I was growing up. Even then my exposure to the ministry was limited to Wednesday and Sunday.

So I decided early in my seminary education to take as many practical theology classes as possible. I thought these would fill in the gaps in the things that I knew little about. No one ever told me pastoral ministry was much more than preaching, teaching, and ideological enthusiasm. I thought earning a Master of Divinity degree from a respected school would grant to me a certain level of immediate respect.

During my seminary education I discovered expository preaching and teaching to be one of my strengths. Therefore, I took huge strides in being theologically sound, practical, and alive in the pulpit. My earlier life experiences helped me to develop leadership and administrative skills.

I felt like the prophet Isaiah, "Here am I Lord, send me."

At the foundation of these characteristics was a heart that beat for the kingdom of God. I had high ideals. I wanted to be used as a change agent in the lives of people. I was ready to conquer any obstacle, so I thought. In this zeal, naiveté, and self-deception I went to my first church in the fall of 1983.

I grew up in a Presbyterian church where I was taught to address the minister respectfully as "Reverend" or "Pastor." But soon I felt like Rodney Dangerfield. I got no respect.

About 90 percent of the congregation, even the children, called me everything but "Pastor." There was one man who called me PM (Pastor Mike).

These people didn't care about what I had studied until they knew what I cared about. I thought they would be willing and ready to accept my new and creative ideas. Was I in for a surprise! After all, they told me they wanted to grow. But how fast and in what areas were never defined.

I had moved from urban Chicago to rural America, from cement and skyscrapers to the rolling countryside, punctuated with barns and silos. From the smell of exhaust to the smell of manure. From the hectic pace of stop-and-go traffic to a town with only three stoplights.

My people all had different priorities and unwritten agendas. Nevertheless, I gallantly marched into my first pastorate with the strengths and knowledge of a graduate-level education as well as a high level of naiveté and a generous amount of ignorance.

In that church I was continually challenged on ridiculous issues that eventually eroded my self-worth. J. Oswald Sanders, in his book *Spiritual Leadership,* says, "There is nothing else that so kills the efficiency, capability, and initiative of a leader as destructive criticism. Its destructive effect cannot be underestimated. It tends to hamper and undercut the efficiency of a man's thinking process. It chips away at his self-respect and undermines his confidence in his ability to cope with his responsibilities."

For example, during one of our quarterly business meetings, one woman challenged the meaning of the pastor as "ex officio" member of boards and committees as it was written in the bylaws of the church. She wanted me to understand I had no reason to attend the Christian Education committee meeting or any other committee meetings. If I wanted to know what went on, I should read the minutes.

Why did I ever come here? I thought. *How could the sweetness turn so sour?*

After five years of ministry, with tears in my eyes, I resigned as pastor of that church. For some it was a glorious day, for others a very sad day. The people in that church gave me experiences I will never forget.

In those first five years of ministry, sandwiched in between the deaths of both my parents, I encountered within the church body two cases of incest, two attempted suicides, a runaway, several divorces, a convicted drug dealer, a case involving a woman whose actions resulted in the death of a six-month-old baby, and wife abuse. By the fourth year in the ministry I was exhausted.

During the last two years of my ministry, I was running on the treadmill of busyness. I thought this made me more important. I had stopped listening to my inner voice as well as the counsel from others. I had stopped taking personal inventory of my life and ministry! I began just going through the motions. I soon began to relinquish all extracurricular activities. I resigned from the board of directors of the Crisis Pregnancy Center, relinquished my responsibilities as the devotion coordinator for the *Evening Times,* and preached less at area nursing homes. I needed to rest.

Finally, after I resigned, I moved my family back to Chicago, into the house where I grew up. I busied myself by painting, plumbing, landscaping, and doing various other jobs. I was running away from the hurt, the failure, and my feelings.

At this point the synthesis began. I began to sort out the pieces. The rush of the pastorate clouded my perception of the reality of human nature, which over time had produced a deep hurt, resentment, anger, and the crushing of my spirit. I didn't have the resources or the capacity to handle the dilemmas that I personalized because of how God wired me. I stopped believing in myself and began questioning the biblical convictions that once shaped my life. I was tired of constantly being challenged by "well-intentioned dragons." I told myself that pastoral ministry was not a hundred-yard dash but a marathon. I never expected to hit heartbreak hill so soon.

As I reflect on my experience, I can now begin to understand why I had such difficulty. I am a person who likes to make favorable impressions. I looked for recognition from people, which has caused anxiety for me at times. I am prone to understand feelings before understanding the facts. Sometimes I feel people don't like me for ridiculous reasons. Couple this with the hard realities of ministry and the decisions that we need to make, and the result is heartbreaking.

I am beginning to understand the need for personal recognition as the motivating factor behind my actions. I talked to many different people, and it became easy for me to hear what I wanted to hear. The proverb, "Faithful are the wounds of a friend," was difficult for me to swallow.

The obvious problem with needing approval comes in the area of personal growth. I now understand I need a good balance of encouragement and objective criticism. This will help keep me focused on the objectives at hand so I continue to become a more usable vessel for our Lord.

As a pastor I had difficulty understanding various types of leaders in the church, that everyone was not going to lead like me. Instead of drawing upon the strengths of others, I considered them a threat to my style of leadership and to my personality.

In order to build a team, I now understand the need for a variety of people. We need each other. I believe this is the very idea Paul was talking about when he mentions the gifts of the Spirit in 1 Corinthians 12, Romans 12, and Ephesians 4. Some team members will be more noticeable than others but all are needed and important.

This is an exciting time in my life. I am experiencing self-discovery, who I am in the body of Christ. I can now look back and see how I blew it and made some bad choices because I needed approval and recognition from others. I can say with confidence that I have matured. I am gaining a better understanding of myself as well as the ministry. I feel good about who I am and what I am doing.

As I periodically take a personal inventory, I am becoming softer clay in the Potter's hands. I am becoming more usable for the kingdom and less uptight about myself. I know this is a lifelong process. I am thankful for this place in my life.

A. W. Tozer was right when he said, "It is highly doubtful that God can use anyone greatly until he has been crushed deeply." The crushing isn't over. At times putting the pieces back together is more painful than the crushing.

The solutions to the issues that bombard us can't be bottled up and sold to us when we are thirsty and in need of relief. My early years of ministry might have been easier if that were true.

Thomas Merton wrote,

> Many poets are not poets for the same reason that many religious men are not saints: they never succeed in being themselves. They waste their years in vain efforts to be some other poet, some other saint. They wear out their minds and bodies in a hopeless endeavor to have somebody else's experience or write somebody else's poems or possess somebody else's sanctity. They want quick success and they are in such a haste to get it that they cannot take time to be true to themselves. And when the madness is upon them they argue that their very haste is a species of integrity.[1]

How then shall we regard the role of theology as we work at becoming true to ourselves?

I consider the full scope of our Christianity to be certain beliefs, convictions, and attitudes that determine our lifestyles as well as lay the foundation for appropriate decision making. The development of a personal theology is not an isolated experience. As rapid changes affect our society, they begin to affect the church. Even so, the authority of Scripture remains the same, an authoritative witness that serves as "a lamp to my feet and a light for my path" (Ps. 119:105).

The theological tension for today's minister is both ethical and devotional. The primary experience of the minister becomes the actual living out and personal practice of his or her doctrinal belief system. The ethical maze ministers face daily tests the rigidity or tenacity of their belief system. For some, their belief systems will continue to speak of the Bible as a dictator in the decision-making process. This legalistic approach to Scripture reduces the Word to a collection of rules, laws, and principles that formulate the commands of God to every situation for every age.

For example, a well-known pastor from whom I sought advice firmly believed that Jesus' words "to love one another" took precedence over any form of church discipline or social protest. He believed this to such a degree that when the need for moral and ethical decision making was obvious, he would overlook the situation. When social action was necessary, he abstained because he felt his actions were unloving.

At first I could not understand his reasoning. Later I realized his theology was so intertwined with his personal experience and temperament that he could not objectively consider any other theological options. His ethical framework was set in the default mode as an integration between the Judeo-Christian ethic and the conscience ethic.

On the other hand, maybe he was afraid of confrontation and buttressed that fear with theological constructs.

The authority of the Bible in Christian ethics is focused precisely in the fact that it is the primary source for shaping the church's understanding of the nature of the Christian life. This is true in three primary ways: (1) shaping Christian identity, (2) the formation of Christian character, and (3) guidance for decision making.[2]

The role of theology is crucial. I hope my studies will cause ministers to examine what they believe about various issues and why, in order to raise the concept of ethical awareness. The integration between theology and practice is essential for the building up of the body of Christ.

For some, even the thought of practicing something other than Christian love or truth telling, regardless of the consequences, seems to be moral compromise.

The Christian life is a life lived by principles, principles drawn from the character of God via sacred Scriptures. We fight a war on two fronts, meeting two perplexing difficulties. Our first problem is to discern the good. Our second problem is to muster the moral courage to do the good.[3]

The knowledge provided by ethics supplies weapons for only half the moral struggles we face.

The foundation of the Christian life is the inspired Word of God. The hope for ministers is that an omniscient God has gone before us. The dilemmas that daily confront the pastor require a certain amount of confidence and risk. I trust what I have experienced and written will not be considered purely anthropocentric. On the contrary, I aspire to stimulate ministers to consider biblical authority as the center of all things and the plumb line by which questionable ethics can be determined. Ethics implies the existence of authority.

Reinhold Niebuhr called the injunctions of the Gospels "impossible possibilities." It is true that for Christians, one answer to the ethical question of secrecy and confidentiality boils down to, "How much shall I keep and how much shall I give away?"[4]

Presently, as I minister at Moody Church, I periodically receive phone calls from pastors, parishioners, and even pastors' wives who are faced with personal dilemmas. They are looking for solutions or, for some, just a listening ear, because that seems to be the only type of momentary resolution. Their stories are filled with pain, confusion, and hurt. They know the Word and for many their dilemmas have paralyzed them, preventing them from considering any options other than the sometimes narrow framework they have practiced. The integration of the Word of God should move us beyond merely quoting the canon of Scripture unconsciously.

The time has come for ministers to consider and implement a framework that gives the leadership of our churches options for practicing professional moral ethics. In so doing the body of Christ will be less prone to suffer from the attacks of the Enemy. The pastor today is under severe attack from not only the pressure of the world but also the pressure of having a successful church. It is a wise pastor who knows that "since there is so much that is evil and vicious in human society which leaves out of account its creaturely answerability to the almighty God, the ethical situation is far from being simple and straightforward."[5]

Ours is a calling from God to be carried out in His power through the wisdom of His Word and the minds He has given us. "Even when informed by Christian faith and illuminated by Scripture, there will always be issues and decisions that remain ambiguous."[6]

Sometime, somewhere in pastoral ministry the ethical baton will be passed. Some will let it drop, others will just grab it and run without looking, but those who choose the "road less traveled" will pray, seek God's wisdom, and reach carefully in order that they may grab responsibly what God has given them. The brevity and frailty of life is too precious for arriving at judgment in a brief moment, out of ignorance. May His will be done.

CHAPTER ELEVEN

PUTTING IT INTO PRACTICE

THE KAHNS WERE NEW TO Hardwood Community Church. They had been in the United States for several years after coming from the Middle East and were finally able to purchase a condominium in their city. Pastor Alex was pleased to see Rhada and her three children in church because they brought some ethnic diversity and a different cultural perspective to the other members of the church. The children seemed to adjust well to the Sunday school and youth group. Everyone seemed more interested in their personal background and previous life than in wondering why Rhada's husband didn't attend church with the rest of the family. Pastor Alex had met him once at a church social soon after the family first started attending, but that was the only time.

One Tuesday morning, unannounced, Rhada stopped by the church office and asked if she could speak with Pastor Alex. She seemed visibly shaken, so the secretary gave her a cup of coffee and alerted Pastor Alex. Shortly, he ushered her into his office. A little confused by her visit, he boldly said, "Rhada, I am surprised by your visit. What can I do for you?" With those words Rhada began to sob; the tears streamed down her cheeks. Pastor Alex quickly gave her some tissue and let her cry before probing a little more.

"What seems to be bothering you today?" He asked.

Rhada responded, "Not just today, several times a week, but Pastor Alex if I tell you please don't let anyone know I was here or spoke to you. Things will only get worse. Please, please understand what I am saying."

Pastor Alex wasn't sure he could give his word on this one. "Well Rhada, I can't say I won't tell anyone, but I want to let you know I will try to understand you and if I can help you with whatever it is, I will."

That pleased Rhada. She regained her composure and began to fill Pastor Alex in on all the details. In her family's culture, men are superior to women, make all the decisions, and can treat their families any way they like, even if it appears abusive to other cultures. Rhada's husband was stressed out at work. Regularly, after coming home from work, he would take his anger out on the family, slapping, hitting, and pushing her and the children. Some days the bruises were worse than others. For several months the family walked on egg shells day after day, never knowing when his temper would boil over. She had nowhere to go. If her husband found out that someone else knew, the situation at home would only get worse. Not only that, for some reason he didn't mind them going to church. It gave him several hours of peace and quiet on Sunday morning.

"Pastor Alex," Rhada said, "we love coming to this church. We have made friends here, but I don't know what to do. That is why I have come to you. I want my husband to become a Christian so badly but don't know what to say or how to do it. Is there some way you can help my situation without making it worse for my family?" What is Pastor Alex to do? Should he confront the husband? acknowledge Rhada's pain and forget she ever said anything? discuss it with the elders of the church and seek their insight? These are the challenges that lay ahead for Pastor Alex. Let's consider how we can come up with some possible solutions that will benefit Rhada, her children, and her husband as we put this dilemma through the Decision-Making Tower. Let's put our learning into practice.

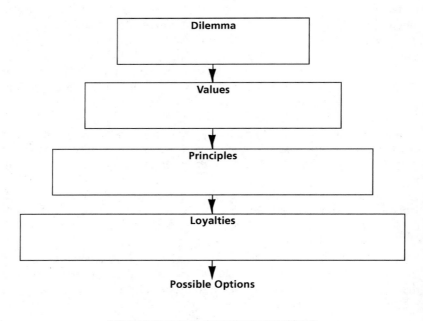

CHILD ABUSE PREVENTION POLICIES

CHURCH WORKER'S POLICY

Grace Bible Chapel
52 NW 7th Avenue
Grand Rapids, Minnesota 55744

Grace Bible Chapel has adopted this Church Worker's Policy for a variety of reasons.

1. We want our church to be a safe place for children and this policy will help us do that.
2. We want anyone who works with us to feel that we are doing everything possible to protect them and their reputation.
3. We want to protect our church and staff and workers from accusations and lawsuits.
4. We are following the recommendations of our insurance carrier to better protect everyone involved in our church activities and to provide for continued insurance coverage.

This policy will apply to all pastoral staff, elders, deacons, Sunday school teachers, AWANA leaders, Grace Christian School personnel, nursery help, Junior Church, Release Time teachers, MOPS, camp personnel or anyone else, including substitutes, who has contact with Grace Bible Chapel ministry or programs.

The effective date will be June 1, 1996 for all elders and deacons, and September 1 for all others.

APPLICATION PROCESS:
1. Each applicant must be an active or associate member of Grace Bible Chapel.

Policies used by permission of the churches.

2. A Basic Information Sheet must be filled out and returned either to Pastor or the Christian Education Director. These sheets will be held in a locked file and will be available only to the pastor, Children Education Director and Vice-Chairman of the Board of Elders.
3. An interview will be held with either the pastor or Christian Education Director.
4. Final approval will be by the Elder Board and the applicant's name will be added to a list of those approved as a church worker. All ministries will be limited to using only people on that list.

PROCEDURES:
1. There will always be two adults in each room.
2. The door of the room must be open unless there is a window in the room.
3. The same rule applies to any church-related activities away from the church building.

REPORTING:
Because any church worker is considered a mandated reporter, the following steps should be taken if you see or hear anything that might indicate a child is being, or has been, physically or sexually abused. Report what you saw or heard immediately to either the pastor or the Christian Education Director. As soon as possible, write up a report with all the pertinent information and get that to the pastor or Christian Education Director. You are protected by law from having your name disclosed to the parties involved. The pastor or Christian Education Director will be responsible for reporting to the proper authorities.

Approved: Elder Board

GRACE BIBLE CHAPEL

Basic informational sheet for all staff and workers serving or
desiring to serve in ministry at the Chapel

Thank you for filling out this form. It is not a contract for employment nor does it constitute a commitment of the Chapel or administration to the person filling it out.

BASIC INFORMATION: (Please print)

Name _____

Address _____

Telephone _____ Date of birth _____

Are you a born-again Christian?   Yes _____ No _____

Please give a short account of your conversion to Christ _____
_____
_____
_____

Are you now serving in ministry at Grace Bible?   Yes _____ No _____

Are you a church member?   Yes _____ No _____ If so, where? _____

Pastor's name _____

Address _____

Telephone _____

Have you read and are you in complete agreement with the Constitution/Bylaws
and Statement of Faith of Grace Bible Chapel?   Yes _____ No _____

Position applied for _____

Position in which you are now serving _____

List previous church work involving children/youth

               Role   Church   Location
_____
_____
_____

List additional ministry experiences and/or education that have prepared you
for children's youth work _____
_____
_____
_____

Which age group do you prefer to work with?
Infants 0–6 months _____   Infants 7–12 months _____
Toddlers 12–24 months _____   Toddlers 24–36 months _____
4-yr.-olds _____   5-yr.-olds _____   1st–3rd grade _____
4th–6th grade _____   7th–8th grade _____   9th–12th grade _____
Adults _____

Are there any physical or personal reasons that might limit your full
participation in ministry (family, professional, and/or personal responsibilities)?
Yes _____   No _____

If so, please explain _____

_____

_____

Churches today have a LEGAL RESPONSIBILITY to ask certain questions of all workers and personnel concerning their backgrounds. All information will be kept in strictest confidence as it may relate to those LEGAL requirements. Insurance companies are making this a requirement of churches that they insure.

Have you ever been charged with and/or convicted of a felony?
Yes _____ No _____
Explain _____

_____

Have you ever been charged with and/or convicted of child abuse or a crime involving actual or attempted sexual molestation of a minor? Yes _____ No _____
Explain_____

_____

Have you ever been physically or sexually abused?   Yes _____ No _____
Explain_____

_____

In all good faith I certify that the above information is true and complete to the best of my knowledge.

Name (please print) _____

Signature _____ Date submitted _____

Interview date _____ Signature of interviewer _____

Approved _____ Date _____

CHILDREN'S AND YOUTH MINISTRY POLICIES

First Evangelical Free Church
1407 Kate Shelley Drive
Boone, IA 50036

Information for Children's or Youth Ministry

Thank you for your interest in helping to nurture children or youth here at First EFC. The mission of Children's Ministry at First EFC is to share God's Word and God's love with children of all ages and their families, so that they can have a relationship with Him, and to nurture them toward maturity in Him. Our youth Ministry strives to create a place where teens can be reached by God, be challenged to commit their lives to Him, and be equipped to reach others for Him.

Our desire is to protect children from all abuse in whatever form, but we believe that sexual abuse is probably the most damaging form of abuse that can happen to a child. We will focus our policies and procedures primarily on that form of abuse. In order to do that we need to provide an environment that will

1. safeguard children and youth from sexual molestation;
2. protect church staff and volunteer workers from potential allegations of sexual abuse;
3. limit the extent of our church's legal risk and liability due to sexual abuse.

Because of your interest in working with children or youth, we are requesting that you complete this information form and return it as soon as possible.

Answers to Some Questions You May Be Asking

- What has happened to make this process necessary?

As child abuse cases continue to increase in today's society, our church has a responsibility to protect our children from that risk in every way possible. We are grateful to God that He has protected us from those incidents, but we are also not naive. We know the enemy will try to harm our church in any way possible, including such an occurrence. God has entrusted to us the care of His children, who are created in His image. Through prayer and implementation of this screening process we endeavor to trust God and strive to reduce the risk in the church.

- Who has to complete this process and why do we have to complete it?

All paid staff and those volunteers who work with children or youth will complete this Information Form for Children's or Youth Ministry. This form needs to be completed for the three reasons listed above, which are to safeguard children and adults and to address questions of liability for insurance purposes.

- How will it be determined whether an individual is approved to work in children's or youth ministry?

We are committed to having individuals serve who believe in Jesus as their Savior and Lord and live that out in their daily lives; who have no record of previous conviction of any type of abuse; who complete all the appropriate forms, agreeing to abide by the policies and doctrinal statement of the church; and who agree to be interviewed by the appropriate people in the course of their ministry.

- What about confidentiality?

This form and any other information received will be kept strictly confidential and will be available to the appropriate pastor(s) and those conducting the interview. Each file will be kept in a secure location after the process is completed.

- What can I do to help?

Abide by all the policies found in the Children's and Youth Ministry Policies, including those listed below.

Follow the "two adult" rule (two adults will be present whenever ministry is taking place with children or youth). This rule reduces the risk of sexual molestation and also reduces the risk of false accusations of molestation, which can be equally devastating.

Obtain parental permission before going out alone with a child or spending time alone with a child in an unsupervised situation.

Use the Nursery Identification procedure. Children should only be released to properly identified and pre-authorized adults.

Discuss suspicious behavior, allegations, or symptoms of child abuse immediately with the designated and appropriate individual. Any inappropriate conduct or relationships between an adult worker and a member of the youth group or a child should be reported, confronted immediately, and investigated.

NOTE: Before completing the following form, it is important that you can answer this question:

"Do I understand why we are going through this process?"

Thank you for your cooperation in providing a safe and secure environment in which children and youth can be ministered to for the glory of God.

CONFIDENTIAL

Name _____ Birth date _____ Phone _____

Address _____

Occupation _____ Business phone _____

1. In what area of ministry or with what age would you like to work, and why you would like to work in that area of ministry?

2. What spiritual gifts and abilities do you have that would be a benefit in the ministry in which you desire to be involved? List any previous training or experience (church or non-church related) you have had working with children or youth, including location and dates, in the last five years.

3. How long have you been attending First EFC of Boone? _____
Are you a member?   YES   NO   Where did you previously attend and what were the ministries in which you were involved?

4. When did you become a Christian? _____ Please explain your relationship with Christ by telling how being a Christian affects your daily life, citing Scripture on which you base your salvation (use back side of sheet if necessary).

5. In order that we may better provide training, what needs do you perceive you have that may be addressed to increase your effectiveness with children or youth?

NOTE: We are compelled to ask the next two questions in order to protect the children and youth in our ministry and in order to better serve the applicant. If you prefer, answers to these questions below may be discussed directly with the supervising pastor involved in this process.

6. Have you ever been convicted of child sexual abuse, physical abuse, incest, sexual molestation, improper advancements or improprieties?   YES   NO

If yes, please explain.

7. Have you ever been the victim of sexual abuse?   YES   NO

Children's and Youth Ministry Policies

1. Two adults shall be present whenever ministry is taking place with children or youth.
2. Parental permission shall be obtained when transporting children and youth to and from church ministries; when having overnights or other outings; when spending one-on-one time with students.
3. Follow the nursery identification system when working in the nursery or leaving children in the nursery.
4. Check with your ministry leader before you allow someone to help or visit in your classroom.
5. Report any suspicious activity immediately to your ministry leader and/or pastor.
6. All church staff and children's/youth ministry volunteers will complete a Ministry Information Form, will sign the church statement of faith, agree to abide by the church's policies, and be interviewed.
7. Use discretion when demonstrating affection with a child.
8. Force shall not be used with children unless it is to restrain a child from hurting another or in self-defense.
9. All who desire to be involved in children's or youth ministry shall first be faithful attendees of the services of the church weekly for at least six months and be actively supportive of the church and its ministries.

This information in this form is correct to the best of my knowledge.

Should my form be accepted, I agree to be bound by the bylaws and policies of First Evangelical Free Church of Boone and to refrain from unscriptural conduct in the performance of my services on behalf of First Evangelical Free Church of Boone.

I further state that I HAVE CAREFULLY READ THE FOREGOING RELEASE AND KNOW THE CONTENTS THEREOF AND I SIGN THIS RELEASE AS MY OWN FREE ACT. This is a legally binding agreement which I have read and understand.

I am willing that a photocopy of this authorization be accepted with the same authority as the original.

_____
Signature   Date

_____
Driver's License #   SSN #   State of issue

_____   _____
   witness (for verification)   witness (for verification)

PLEASE BE SURE TO SIGN THIS IN THE PRESENCE OF TWO OTHER PEOPLE.

Procedural Guidelines for reporting suspected child abuse involving children in the care of the First EFC of Boone ministries.

1. Every allegation should be treated as sincere and legitimate. Whoever receives a complaint should listen calmly and carefully, noting the child's behavior. Don't panic, don't overreact to the information disclosed. Don't criticize or suggest the child is not telling the truth. Respect and protect the child's privacy by not having the conversation become the topic of discussion with others. Do not deny or minimize the allegation or blame the victim.

2. Refer the situation and the child to one of the designated people* from our church, who will then contact the parent(s)/guardian. All of this should be done within twenty-four hours. The child with the parent(s)/guardian will relate the event to two designated people who will confirm and put in writing what was said for the handwritten Incident Report, in order to establish reasonable cause to believe that abuse has occurred and in order to keep accurate documentation.

3. Two of the designated people will approach the person(s) accused (when the safety of the child is assured) to hear their position on the matter and establish accuracy, according to biblical guidelines (Matthew 18:15–17). Handwritten notes of the meeting will be taken.

4. The designated people will, after steps 1–3 are completed, immediately consult with our attorney and our insurance company. The designated people will, after consulting with the attorney and insurance company, then make the determination as to whether there is reasonable cause to believe abuse has occurred.

5. If a reasonable cause determination has been made these people will be notified:

   County Human Services
   Church Insurance Company

   The church will cooperate with the law enforcement authorities and the Department of Human Services in their investigation of the matter. It is the authorities' responsibility to process the complaint.

6. If a paid employee or volunteer of the church has been accused, that person will be relieved of their ministry duties with pay during the investigation.

7. The church chairman will act as a spokesman for the church. That person will, after consultation with legal counsel, prepare a written statement in advance and respond to all media inquiries. All questions from the public will be addressed only by this person.

8. When deemed prudent, the congregation will be apprised of the allegations. This should be a brief, factual statement to the active members of the church informing them of the allegations. This is so that the congregation does not hear it from outside sources. This is also to encourage the congregation not to talk about this situation outside of the church, as this is how rumors start.

*The Designated People will be a group of four people, two men and two women, who will handle complaints such as this. This group will include the deacon board chairman, a Christian Education Board member, and two other people appointed by the Christian Education board and approved by the General Board.

Approved February 1, 1996
© First Evangelical Free Church of Boone

INFECTIOUS DISEASE/ HIV POLICIES

STATEMENT OF POLICIES AND PROCEDURES REGARDING HUMAN IMMUNODEFICIENCY VIRUS (HIV) AND ACQUIRED IMMUNODEFICIENCY SYNDROME (AIDS).

Church by the Side of the Road
P.O. Box 68545
Seattle, Washington 98168

We, the members of the Church by the Side of the Road, believing the Bible to be the only inspired, infallible, and authoritative Word of God, must respond to the current HIV/AIDS crisis, ministering spiritually, emotionally, and physically to all affected.

We believe that a personal relationship with Jesus Christ can deliver individuals from the power of sin and disease, and we believe that we must minister to all peoples, Christian and non-Christian.

According to the most recent research published, HIV/AIDS virus spreads through infected persons to others by sexual intercourse, direct blood transfer, and intravenous drug use (IV). The virus can also be passed on through organ transplant and from infected mothers to their babies during pregnancy, at birth, or shortly after birth through breast milk.

AIDS is caused by the Human Immunodeficiency Virus. This virus does not survive well outside the body, and therefore is not spread by casual nonsexual contact. This means that you cannot catch HIV from a simple kiss, hug, handshake, cough, sneeze, or similar casual contact. Scientists have not found a single instance where HIV has been transmitted through ordinary nonsexual contact in a family, church, or social setting.

In light of this, we have instituted the following policies for our church.

HIV/AIDS EDUCATION
Proper education can dispel fear, instill hope, and enhance ministry. Therefore we are committed to educating ourselves and our community

---

Policies used by permission of the churches.

regarding HIV/AIDS prevention, transmission, and ministry to those affected. For the purpose of mutual education, we will endeavor to collaborate with other community groups and organizations, making a concerted effort to maintain a current understanding of the HIV situation.

PREMARRIAGE TESTING

Because HIV/AIDS is transmitted sexually and because AIDS is passed on from mother to newborn infant, the pastors and counseling staff of the Church by the Side of the Road are advised to recommend that individuals coming from "high risk" backgrounds be strongly encouraged to secure anonymous testing for HIV and other sexually transmitted diseases, and share those results with their prospective marital partner.

NURSERY

As is now current policy, children with symptoms of illness or who are prone to be biters are to remain with their adult guardian.

Because children from birth until toilet-trained often share bottles and teething implements, those children in this category who have tested positive to HIV are also to remain with their adult guardian, even though the likelihood of transmission is negligible. Older children testing positive are encouraged to participate fully in church activities.

KITCHEN POLICY/FOOD PREPARATION

All individuals who work directly with food preparation and serving must remove themselves from such tasks when there is evidence of any illness or exposed lesions.

EMERGENCIES OR ACCIDENTS

Since some individuals may be carriers of HIV and not even know it, latex gloves should be worn when administering first aid or cleaning up bodily fluids. A specially equipped first-aid kit and a special body fluid spill cleanup kit will be available at all times in the church office. Similar traveling kits will be available for those activities that take place off of the church premises.

CONFIDENTIALITY

As in all personal matters, confidentiality will be maintained by all professionals and lay members of the congregation. Information will be shared only on a need-to-know basis upon agreement by the HIV-positive individual.

Because of the unique nature of this disease, we must affirm our belief in celibacy outside heterosexual marriage, monogamy within marriage, and the honoring of the human body as the temple of the Holy Spirit.

This policy is intended to cover all of our church activities, whether held on the church premises or away.

Officially Adopted February 23, 1993.

INFECTIOUS DISEASE POLICY

The Moody Church
1609 North LaSalle Boulevard
Chicago, Illinois 60614

As Christians, we believe the Bible to be our ultimate authority for our beliefs and behavior. The AIDS epidemic is a call to our members and all of society to return to obedience to the teachings of Scripture. We also believe it is an opportunity to reach out to those who have been infected with this disease because of sinful conduct, as well as those who have been the innocent victims of others' destructive behavior.

Our goal is to help both groups of sufferers understand that Christ invites all to come to Him for forgiveness and acceptance. This policy has been written with the hope that Christ's love will be thoroughly demonstrated in the church.

The policy as stated will be divided into five parts for use in congregational education and guiding programmatic decisions.

PART A.   Introduction
PART B.   A compilation of information from various sources used to guide the Christian Education Committee in its recommendations. Prepared materials and a bibliography are on reserve in the church library.
PART C.   Medical facts about AIDS and our response to the issue as it relates to the various ministries/activities of Moody Church.
PART D.   Recommendations regarding program, personnel, and facilities.
PART E.   Summary and Conclusion

PART A

INTRODUCTION
The Christian Education Committee has been asked by the Elders of Moody church to provide a policy, and procedures, for dealing with HIV infection and/ or AIDS as it pertains to ministries and activities for Moody Church. Based upon the recommendation of the Board of Elders, this policy was passed by the Executive Committee on October 8, 1990.

PART B
A compilation of information from various sources used to guide the Christian Education Committee in its recommendations are on reserve in the church library and are available upon request.

PART C

MEDICAL FACTS
Acquired Immune Deficiency Syndrome (AIDS) is an infection caused by the Human Immunodeficiency Virus (HIV). This virus greatly reduces or sometimes destroys the body's immune system. The immune system is the body's defense system. It is responsible for fighting disease. Because the immune system is

weakened, infections which are normally harmless to a healthy person can be very dangerous or even fatal to a person with AIDS. These normally harmless infections are called opportunistic infections.

It is estimated that more than one million Americans are HIV infected. If the symptoms of infection are mild, the individual has AIDS Related Complex or ARC. When the symptoms become severe and opportunistic infections occur, the individual has AIDS. The time period between being infected with the virus and developing symptoms is called the incubation period. The incubation period for ARC and AIDS can range from a few months to ten years. According to the most recent research published by the Institute of Medicine, National Academy of Sciences, and the American Red Cross, the AIDS virus spreads through infected persons to others by sexual intercourse, direct blood transfer, and intravenous drug use (IV). The virus can also be passed on from infected mothers to their babies during pregnancy, at birth, or shortly after birth.

AIDS is caused by a virus that does not survive well outside the body. The virus is not spread by casual nonsexual contact. Scientists have not found any instance in which the AIDS virus has been transmitted through ordinary nonsexual contact in a family, work, or social setting.

OUR RESPONSE AS IT APPLIES TO THE
VARIOUS MINISTRIES AND ACTIVITIES
AT MOODY CHURCH

In light of the above information, we have instituted the following policies for our church.

While all persons who wish to participate with us at Moody Church will certainly be welcomed, we have instituted universal precautions as established by the Centers for Disease Control (CDC) to minimize the risk of spread of communicable diseases (see Appendix A). As such, **no person who has been diagnosed as being HIV-positive or having AIDS will be excluded from any of the ministries or activities of Moody Church.**

In addition to guidelines established by the CDC, Moody Church lists four additional precautionary measures:

1. Children with weeping sores or aggressive biting behaviors will be remanded to the parent or adult guardian.
2. Parents should bring the child's own toys from home. They will be routinely placed in a cloth bag that will hang from the crib. Cloth bags will be laundered each week. Other toys should be sprayed with Basic-G and wiped after each use.
3. Adult caregivers with weeping sores, cuts, or chapped hands should cover above mentioned and wear latex gloves for additional protection.
4. A form will be available in our children's departments, birth to six years, asking parents the following questions.

(Answering these medical questions is voluntary and is not a condition of enrollment.)

ALL MEDICAL INFORMATION WILL BE KEPT CONFIDENTIAL

Is your child known to have one of the following chronic communicable diseases declared as communicable by the Centers for Disease control (CDC) and/or the Illinois Department of Public Health?

	YES	NO
Hepatitis Type B	_____	_____
Human Immunodeficiency Virus (HIV)	_____	_____
Herpes Simplex Virus	_____	_____
AIDS	_____	_____
Other:	_____	_____

If the child's health condition changes to include a chronic communicable disease, the parent or guardian has the responsibility to notify the director of the department.

Attendance Decision

A decision on attendance shall be based on the following factors:
1. The risk of transmission of the disease to others.
2. The health risk to the particular child.
3. That reasonable accommodations can be made to reduce health risks to the child and others.

This decision will be made based on the best medical/public health information available at the time.

A summary of the child's health problems and care received, as well as his/her physician's recommendations, must be released to the church to assist in the attendance decision. Appropriate medical/public health/legal consultation, including the child's personal physician, will be sought by the church staff person as needed on a case-by-case basis. Medical records may be requested if needed.

PART D

RECOMMENDATIONS REGARDING
PROGRAMS, PERSONNEL, AND FACILITIES

A. The medical condition of a child shall be disclosed only to the extent necessary to minimize the health risks to the child and others. The individual responsible for that ministry will be provided with the appropriate information concerning any special precautions that may be necessary. Moody Church staff members or volunteers shall not disclose the HIV or AIDS status of any individual without the express, written consent and permission of that individual or in the case of a child, their parent, or adult guardian.

B. Post a sign stating a policy regarding children manifesting symptoms of illness. Such a sign will be placed in all Christian Education function locations. The wording of the sign will be as follows:

Parents: Christian Education workers consider the well-being of your child a serious trust. While all persons who wish to participate with us at Moody Church will certainly be welcomed, we have instituted universal precautions as established by the Centers for Disease Control (CDC) to minimize the risk of spread of communicable diseases. As such, no person who has been diagnosed as being HIV-positive or having AIDS will be excluded from any of the ministries or activities of Moody Church. We are committed to keeping you informed concerning these matters and encourage your continued support.

C. No individual will work directly with food preparation and serving when they exhibit physical evidence of a communicable disease, illness, or unbandaged wound or lesion. Cooking and food preparation poses no threat to or from an individual who is HIV-positive or has AIDS.

   Individuals who are HIV positive or have AIDS, but do not evidence any symptoms of a communicable disease, will be allowed to work with food preparation and service.

   All individuals involved in food preparation and service shall begin by thoroughly washing their hands. (Anyone serving food must use disposable serving mittens or gloves.)

D. Train regular Christian Education workers, paid staff, maintenance workers, and volunteers in communicable disease control measures, and require that they administer them routinely, especially when handling blood or bodily fluids from any child (refer to Appendix A).

E. Materials (listed in Appendix A) will be available in all meeting rooms.

F. Ask the Trustees to consider room renovations including:
   1. Sinks with paddle-lever faucets
   2. Antimicrobial treatment in all new carpets
   3. Trash bags, twist-ties, and covered trash cans
   4. Toilet seat cover dispensers in all toilet facilities
   5. Disposable mattress and changing table sheet covers for nursery/toddlers

PART E
SUMMARY AND CONCLUSIONS

A. We believe that responses to AIDS and other infectious diseases will change as circumstances change. This policy will be reviewed and updated as needed.

B. We believe the AIDS epidemic is not only a medical crisis and a national public health emergency, it is also a spiritual challenge. Therefore, we suggest the following proactive ministries:
   1. Explore the implementation of a "Family Class" for families with or without AIDS children who desire their children to be kept under their own supervision during Sunday school and church time.
   2. Investigate interest in starting a support group for families with AIDS-infected children (immediate and extended families).
   3. Encourage a volunteer program of visitation to children who are hospitalized or home-bound with chronic or terminal illnesses to bring to them a gospel message, materials from their class, a special gift, and

greetings from their classmates and teachers. Our continuing adult visitation program could minister to adults.

C. We believe issues of life and death, and proclaiming life in the face of death, have always been primary for the church. To help someone die in circumstances that surround him/her with loving support is definitely a challenge that is already part of the ministry of the church. Our ministry with the dying is, without question, one that should be extended to the person with AIDS. In whatever ways we minister to persons with AIDS or other diseases, we need to remember that we are called upon to do more than help the HIV-infected person "die well." We are called upon to witness about Jesus Christ who proclaimed life even in the midst of death. Christ gave His life so that all who believe in Him might be renewed into fellowship with God. We witness to this relationship through our actions to bind up wounds, to sit at bedsides and listen without fear or judgment, and to bring this message to those who are suffering.

POLICY ON AIDS

College Church of Wheaton
Wheaton, Illinois 60187

I. MEDICAL FACTS

Acquired Immunodeficiency Syndrome (AIDS) caused by Human Immunodeficiency Virus (HIV) is an infectious disease for which there is no known cure. Persons who develop the full spectrum of the disease become tragically ill and, to date, invariably die. A person may be infected with the virus for up to ten years without symptoms. During this time, the person is contagious but may be totally unaware of the infection. It has become a significant problem in our country as well as in the rest of the world. According to current medical knowledge, the Human Immunodeficiency Virus is not highly contagious by casual contact. It is not transmitted through a kiss, hug, or handshake, nor is it transmitted by mosquitoes or on toilet seats. It is highly transmittable in the following ways:

A. Sexual intercourse, both homosexual and heterosexual with an infected partner

B. Use of contaminated needles or other instruments, especially as in intravenous drug use

C. Blood transfusions of infected blood, blood products, and clotting factors (for hemophiliacs), especially prior to 1983 when such products were not screened for the HIV virus

D. Intrauterine transfer from an infected mother to an unborn infant

II. SCRIPTURAL PRINCIPLES

A. Biblical Sexuality

As Christians we believe the Bible to be authoritative for all faith and practice. Therefore, we accept all Scripture and biblical principles to be authoritative in relation to human sexuality and the proper care of our bodies. We hold as unacceptable behavior:

1. All homosexuality (Romans 1:24–27)
2. Heterosexual relations (as relating to a man and a woman) outside of marriage (1 Corinthians 6:19)
3. Drug abuse (1 Corinthians 3:16–17)

We affirm our belief in:

1. Heterosexual marriage (Genesis 2:24)
2. Abstinence outside a marriage (1 Corinthians 6:19)
3. Faithfulness to one's spouse (Hebrews 13:4)
4. The body as the temple of the Holy Spirit (1 Corinthians 6:19)

B. Christian Ministry

As Christians, we believe we are called to be God's ambassadors of the "Good News" as well as agents of helping and healing to our world (Matt. 25:34–40). We believe that we should love and minister to people regardless of their behavior or circumstances. While we correctly judge heterosexual intercourse outside marriage and all homosexual intercourse as sin, we advocate that Christians refrain from cultivating a judgmental spirit. Whether an individual has contracted AIDS through a sinful lifestyle or by another means of transmission, we believe that ostracism, censoriousness, avoidance, or desertion are wholly unacceptable as Christian responses. Our response will be one of compassion and inclusion. We resolve to follow the example of our Lord who willingly crossed barriers, touched lepers, accepted risks, and identified with all people.

III. POLICIES

A. College Church in Wheaton desires to establish policies and procedures which will fulfill the following three priorities:

1. As a Christ-centered, compassionate church, we wish to offer support, caring, and an opportunity to worship to all people including those who are infected with HIV.
2. We desire to protect those infected with HIV from additional infectious disease.
3. We desire to protect the uninfected church attenders from undue risk of contracting the virus.

B. To these ends, we have established the following policies. Procedural guidelines will also be drawn up to help in the implementation of these policies.

1. AIDS Advisory Council

   The person(s) in our advisory council will be appointed by the pastors. The council will coordinate ministry to the person(s) with AIDS and will make any medical decisions needed.

2. Confidentiality

   The church leadership (i.e. pastoral staff and elders) will maintain confidentiality about an individual who tests positive for HIV, unless the individual is engaged in behavior that is putting others at risk. Any

person who persists in dangerous or unbiblical behavior will come under discipline of the church.
3. Nursery
   Because young children from birth until they are toilet-trained often bite, share bottles and pacifiers, and require diaper changing, those children who have tested positive for HIV might not be permitted in the nursery. Decisions will be made on a case-by-case basis. Every effort will be made to care for infants in the church setting.
4. Children's Programs
   a. Children who test positive for HIV and who are toilet-trained are welcome to attend Sunday school and all church functions and are encouraged to participate fully. They may have access to bathrooms, drinking fountains, etc.
   b. HIV-positive children who lack control over bodily functions, have open wounds or cuts, or display behavior such as biting, may be screened and temporarily excluded. This decision will be made by the AIDS Advisory Council.
   c. Parents of all children who attend College Church are asked to keep their children home if they have a contagious illness. This will prevent the spread of disease to all children, especially the child with AIDS.
5. Adult Programs
   Adults who are HIV-positive are warmly welcomed into our congregation and they should expect to be treated with Christian love and care. This does not diminish our stand regarding unbiblical sexual behavior or drug use. Adults who test HIV-positive may be asked to refrain from certain areas of service. Each case will be decided by the AIDS Advisory Council.
6. Premarital Testing
   The pastoral staff and elders of the church retain the right to require testing for HIV in persons seeking to be married in College Church who are deemed "high risk" for AIDS. This is to protect the potential partner in such a marriage.
7. Education
   College Church is committed to teaching the sanctity of monogamous heterosexual marriage and the dangers of sexual immorality. We will assist parents in the instruction of their children and continue sex education programs already in the Christian Education curriculum, including information regarding AIDS and HIV infections.
8. Ministry to Those with AIDS
   As need grows within the congregation and community, College Church is committed to ministering specifically to people who are affected by this terrible disease.

COMMUNICABLE DISEASE GUIDELINES
Calvary Church
Grand Rapids, Michigan

The following communicable disease guidelines shall apply to church education programs, e.g., nursery, Sunday school, and children's church.

1. People with contagious diseases (spread by casual contact) must remain home until symptoms are gone. Contagious diseases include, but are not limited to, the following:

Chicken pox	Pinkeye
Common cold	Ringworm
Influenza	Scarlet fever
Measles	Strep throat
Mumps	Whooping cough

2. People with diseases not spread by casual contact—When reliable evidence or information from a qualified source confirms that a person is known to have a communicable disease or infection that is known not to be spread by casual contact, i.e. AIDS, Hepatitis B, and other like diseases, or the person is HIV positive, the decision as to whether the infected person will be permitted to attend church educational programs will be made on a case-by-case basis by a review panel.

3. Universal procedures and sanitation—Irrespective of the presence of a disease, routine procedures for handling blood and body fluids will be followed, and adequate sanitation facilities will be available. All teachers, workers, and volunteers working in all education programs, ushers, and all custodial personnel will be trained in the proper procedures for handling blood and body fluids, and these procedures will be strictly adhered to.

4. Instruction—Instruction on the principal modes by which communicable diseases including, but not limited to, Acquired Immunodeficiency Syndrome (AIDS), are spread and the best methods for the restriction and prevention of these diseases shall be provided to all Christian education workers, teachers, and volunteers. These personnel must know that the AIDS virus is not easy to catch, that the best medical knowledge indicates that it is transmitted through the exchange of blood or semen by infected sexual partners, contaminated needles, contaminated blood, or by infected mothers to their infants.

5. Communication—These guidelines will be shared with all church staff, board members, teachers, volunteers, workers, ushers, as well as the congregation at large.

6. Procedures—The person with AIDS, who is HIV positive or having other communicable diseases, will be treated the same as any other individual providing he/she does not pose any threat to the health and safety of others attending church educational programs.

PATTERNS PREDICTING PASTORAL INFIDELITY

Copyright © 1995 by Dave Carder

This survey is a nonscientific instrument highlighting patterns that appear regularly in the lives of pastors who have been involved in infidelity. It is not intended to predict who will definitely become sexually immoral, and it should not be interpreted as a necessarily reliable or valid indicator of those who are struggling with sexual temptation. Furthermore, it does not claim to discriminate between those who have committed adultery and those who might do so in the future. Its usefulness as a screening device is also, as yet, undetermined. This survey is designed to help you evaluate your personal history and lifestyle for parallels with those who have been involved in adultery.

This evaluation form applies only to men. No effort has been made to include information from interviews of females who have had affairs. This evaluation only helps to identify a high-risk group of males who, given the right combination of unfinished business in their lives, lifestyle pattern, and current psychosocial stressors, would be prone to having an affair.

PERSONAL AND FAMILY HISTORY

1. Did you grow up in a family that used a substantial amount of alcohol?
   Yes _____ No _____

2. Were your parents strict disciplinarians, possibly abusive at times?
   Yes _____ No _____

3. Were you sexually molested as a child?
   Yes _____ No _____

4. Did you experience early adolescent heterosexual activity with an older partner (baby-sitter, older sister's friend, and so on)?
   Yes _____ No _____

5. Were you involved in pornography prior to puberty (magazines, video)?
   Yes _____ No _____

6. While you were living at home, were either of your parents involved in an extramarital affair?
   Yes _____ No _____

LIFESTYLE PATTERNS
Please score the following criteria to answer questions 7–24. The higher the score, the truer the statement.

7. As an adolescent I did not get along with authority figures, and I continue to have conflict with the law and/or my supervisors.

   1   2   3   4   5

8. I feel driven, unable to relax and/or to have fun.

   1   2   3   4   5

9. My self-control and anger management skills are strengths in my life.

   1   2   3   4   5

10. I like testing the limits that surround me, e.g., the speed limits, tax and banking laws, church policies, and so on.

    1   2   3   4   5

11. I enjoy getting through a project so that I can get on with the next one. It is important to me to have a number of projects "waiting in line" for my attention.

    1   2   3   4   5

12. I feel alone even in my marriage and am unable to share my fears, deepest feelings, and the longings of my heart with my spouse.

    1   2   3   4   5

13. I recognize in myself the tendency toward compulsive behavior with different things at different times (e.g., food, exercise, work, saving money or spending money, fast driving, and so on).

    1   2   3   4   5

14. I have lots of acquaintances and appear to be close to my family members, but I don't have an intimate friend.

    1   2   3   4   5

15. I like to win and would be described as a fierce competitor in whatever I do.

    1   2   3   4   5

16. My dating life was marked by a series of broken relationships that were ended by me.

    1   2   3   4   5

17. I feel stressed out, almost numb, from all the demands of the ministry upon me.

    1   2   3   4   5

18. I like to be around important people and find myself playing up to relationships with those types of people.

    1   2   3   4   5

19. A review of my financial history contains a series of bounced checks, a large debt-to-income ratio, poor credit, regular use of credit cards to support my lifestyle, and possibly even bankruptcy.

    1   2   3   4   5

20. I have trouble expressing my anger in ways that provide me with relief without wounding others emotionally.

    1   2   3   4   5

21. I don't mind conflict and find that it actually helps me feel better and more in control.

    1   2   3   4   5

22. I like to see what I can get away with by living "close to the edge."

    1   2   3   4   5

23. An area that the Lord has to help me with is a tendency to harbor grudges and a desire for revenge.

    1   2   3   4   5

24. Most of those who know me would say that I am intense, easily irritated, and have high standards of excellence.

    1   2   3   4   5

CIRCUMSTANTIAL FACTORS
Give yourself five points for each of the numbered items you have experienced within the past year.

25. Loss of a close loved one (e.g., child, parent, spouse) _____

26. Suffered a major stressor (e.g., job loss/change, divorce, medical diagnosis/ hospitalization, cross-country move) _____

27. Approached a major life transition (e.g., the birth of a child, mid-life crisis, retirement) _____

TEST-WIDE SCORING
Questions 1–6: "Yes" answers count 10 points each.
If all six questions are answered "yes," give yourself
an additional 40 points.

   Total score for questions 1–6:   _____

Questions 7–14: Total the numbers that you circled.

   Total score for questions 7–24:   _____

Questions 25–27: Give yourself 5 points for
each category experienced.

   Total score for questions 25–27:   _____

   Total Score   _____

EVALUATION OF SCORE

Questions 1–6:   A score over 50 for this section places you in the high-risk group.

Questions 7–24:   A score over 70 for this section places you in the high-risk group.

Total score: A score over 100 is cause for concern. A score of 175 indicates extreme vulnerability to an affair.

A final word. If you find yourself to be in the high-risk category, start working on your family-of-origin issues. If you are married, focus on developing emotional intimacy with your spouse. There are a number of materials available, and the suggestions herein are just a start.

A final warning. High-risk individuals are more vulnerable than they realize. Whatever you do, do not discount your initial score—talk it over with your spouse and start to work on problem areas.[1]

CHAPTER NOTES

Introduction
1. George Barna, *Today's Pastor* (Ventura, Calif.: Regal Books, 1993), 52.
2. Daniel Taylor, "In Pursuit of Character," *Christianity Today* 39, no. 14 (December 11, 1995): 31.
3. Ibid., 33.
4. R. C. Sproul, *Following Christ* (Wheaton, Ill.: Tyndale House, 1983), 8.

Chapter One
1. Walter E. Wiest and Elwyn A. Smith, *Ethics in Ministry: A Guide for the Professional* (Minneapolis: Fortress, 1990), 19.
2. Barna, *Today's Pastor,* 49.
3. Wiest and Smith, *Ethics in Ministry,* 19–34.
4. Walter A. Elwell, ed., *Evangelical Dictionary of Theology* (Grand Rapids: Baker), 377.
5. Jay Jordan-Lake, "Conduct Unbecoming a Preacher," *Christianity Today* 36, no. 2 (February 10, 1992): 8.
6. The principles of this idea originated by Ralph Potter.
7. Ralph Potter, *War and Moral Discourse* (Atlanta: John Knox, 1969), 23ff.
8. Clifford Christians, Kim Rotzell, and Mark Fackler, *Media Ethics: Case Studies and Moral Reasoning,* 2d ed. (New York: Longman, 1987).
9. For a more thorough understanding of your personality style see Keirsey and Bates, *Please Understand Me.*
10. Kenneth S. Kantzer and Carl F. H. Henry, eds., *Evangelical Affirmations* (Grand Rapids: Zondervan, 1990), 201.
11. Ibid., 202–220.
12. Robert N. Beck, ed., *Perspectives in Philosophy* (New York: Holt, Rinehart & Winston, 1975), 18.
13. Ethel Albert, Theodore Denise, and Sheldon Peterfreund, *Great Transitions in Ethics,* 4th edition, (Belmont, Calif.: Wadsworth Publishing, 1980), 227.
14. Sproul, *Following Christ,* 16–17.
15. Christopher Lasch, *The Culture of Narcissism* (New York: W. W. Norton & Company, 1978), 5.
16. Ibid., 53.
17. Reginald Johnson, *Your Personality and the Spiritual Life* (Wheaton, Ill.: Victor Books, 1995), 154–155.
18. Sproul, *Following Christ,* 89.
19. Johnson, *Your Personality and the Spiritual Life,* 32–33.
20. Ibid., 21–29.
21. Ibid., 154–155.

Chapter Two
1. R. K. Bullis and C. S. Mazur, *Legal Issues and Religious Counseling* (Louisville: John Knox, 1993), 90.

2. William A. Teague, "When a Pastoral Colleague Falls," *Leadership* 12, no. 1 (winter 1991): 102–108.
3. Joe E. Trull and James E. Carter, *Ministerial Ethics* (Nashville: Broadman & Holman, 1993), 68–69.
4. Teague, "When a Pastoral Colleague Falls," 109–111.

Chapter Three
1. Marja Mills and Michael Hirsley, "Bible school bars boy, 5, with AIDS," *Chicago Tribune,* 20 April 1990, 1, 19.
2. Maudlyne Ihejirka, "Moody reverses ban; AIDS boy to return to classes," *Chicago Sun-Times,* 21 April 1990, 1, 10.
3. Dr. Patrick Dixon, *The Whole Truth about AIDS* (Nashville: Thomas Nelson, 1989), 147–148.

Chapter Four
1. Editors, "How Common Is Pastoral Indiscretion?" *Leadership* 9, no. 1 (winter 1988): 12–13.
2. Trull and Carter, *Ministerial Ethics,* 81.
3. Editors, "How Common Is Pastoral Indiscretion?" 13
4. John H. Armstrong, *Can Fallen Pastors Be Restored?* (Chicago: Moody Press, 1995), 13.
5. Kenneth Quick, "Confidentiality: Will You Tell Overtures?" *Leadership* 12, no. 3 (summer 1991): 103–105
6. Don Baker, *Beyond Forgiveness* (Portland, Ore.: Multnomah Press, 1984), 33–34.
7. Armstrong, *Can Fallen Pastors Be Restored?* 32.
8. Regrettably, Truman Dollar committed suicide in the spring of 1996.
9. Ed Dobson, "Restoring a Fallen Colleague," *Leadership* 13, no. 1 (winter 1992): 106–121.
10. Armstrong, *Can Fallen Pastors Be Restored?* 34.

Chapter Five
1. Name Withheld, "Speaking the Truth in Safety," *Leadership* 8, no. 3 (summer 1987): 96–97.
2. Ibid., 98.
3. Dann Spader and Gary Mayes, *Growing a Healthy Church* (Chicago: Moody Press, 1991), 73–74.

Chapter Six
1. Quick, "Confidentiality: Will You Tell Overtures?" 104.
2. Rich Van Pelt, *Intensive Care: Helping Teenagers in Crisis* (Grand Rapids: Zondervan, 1988), 69.
3. Candace Walters, *Invisible Wounds* (Portland, Ore.: Multnomah Press, 1987), 93.
4. Ibid., 41–42.
5. Ibid., 87.
6. David J. Atkins, David F. Field, Arthur Holmes, and Oliver O'Donovan, *New Dictionary of Christian Ethics & Pastoral Theology* (Downers Grove, Ill.: InterVarsity Press, 1995), 825.
7. Ibid., 825.
8. R. K. Harrison, ed., *Encyclopedia of Biblical and Christian Ethics* (Nashville: Thomas Nelson, 1987), 398.
9. Earl A. Grollman, *Suicide: Prevention, Intervention, Postvention* (Boston: Beacon Press, 1971), 88.
10. Grollman, *Suicide: Prevention, Intervention, Postvention,* 2d ed. (Boston: Beacon Press, 1988), 123–124.
11. Crisis centers may be listed in the front of your area's phone book. Look under "suicide," "crisis," "mental health," or "counseling." There is also the National Council of Community Mental Health Centers, 6101 Montrose Road, Suite 360, Rockville, MD 20852. They can supply you with those helping professionals in your area.

Chapter Seven
1. Marshall Shelley, *Well-Intentioned Dragons* (Waco, Tex.: *Christianity Today*/Word, 1985), 140–143.

2. William D. Lawrence, *Beyond the Bottom Line* (Chicago: Moody Press, 1994), 30.
3. Kurt D. Bruner, *Responsible Living in an Age of Excuses* (Chicago: Moody Press, 1992), 189–190.

Chapter Eight
1. Charles R. Swindoll, *Sanctity of Life: The Inescapable Issue* (Dallas: Word, 1990), 9.
2. For more information you can write to the Christian Action Council, 422 C Street, N.E., Washington, DC 20002 and ask for the videotape, *Understanding Pregnancy Alternatives.*
3. Curt Young, *The Least of These* (Chicago: Moody Press, 1984), 168.
4. Ibid., 46.
5. Van Pelt, *Intensive Care: Helping Teenagers in Crisis,* 72.
6. Everett L. Worthington Jr., *Counseling for Unplanned Pregnancy and Infertility* (Dallas: Word, 1987), 30.
7. Ibid., 93.
8. Lee Smith, "The New Wave of Illegitimacy," *Fortune,* 18 April 1994, 88.
9. John White, *Eros Defiled* (Downers Grove, Ill.: InterVarsity Press, 1977), 9.
10. Worthington, *Counseling for Unplanned Pregnancy and Infertility,* 94.

Chapter Nine
1. James D. Berkley, *Called into Crisis* (Waco: Word, 1989), 97–102.
2. Hunter Lewis, *A Question of Values* (San Francisco: HarperCollins, 1990), 17–18.
3. Guy Charles, "The Church and the Homosexual," *The Secrets of Our Sexuality,* ed. Gary Collins (Dallas: Word, 1976), 126–127.
4. Baker, *Beyond Rejection* (Portland, Ore.: Multnomah Press, 1985), 62.
5. Greg L. Bahnsen, *Homosexuality: A Biblical View* (Grand Rapids: Baker, 1978), 134.
6. Atkins, Field, Holmes, and O'Donovan, *New Dictionary of Christian Ethics & Pastoral Theology,* 248.
7. Quick, "Confidentiality: Will You Tell Overtures?" 103.
8. Christians, Rotzoll, and Fackler, *Media Ethics: Cases and Moral Reasoning,* 199.
9. Ibid., 248.

Chapter Ten
1. Thomas Merton, *Seeds of Contemplation* (New York: New Directions, 1961), 65.
2. Paul D. Simmons, *Issues in Christian Ethics* (Nashville: Broadman Press, 1980), 29.
3. Sproul, *Following Christ,* 93.
4. Gaylord Noyce, *Pastoral Ethics: Professional Responsibilities of Clergy* (Nashville: Abingdon, 1988), 26.
5. Philip E. Hughes, *Christian Ethics in Secular Society* (Grand Rapids: Baker, 1983), 13.
6. Wiest and Smith, *Ethics in Ministry,* 34.

Appendix Three
1. Dave Carder, Earl Henslin, John Townsend, Henry Cloud, and Alice Brawand, *Secrets of Your Family Tree* (Chicago: Moody Press, 1995), 289–293.

BIBLIOGRAPHY

Albert, E., T. Denise, and S. Peterfruend. *Great Traditions in Ethics*. 4th ed. Belmont, Calif.: Wadsworth, 1980.

Amos, A. E. Jr. "When AIDS Comes to the Church." *Leadership* 10, no. 4 (fall 1989): 67–73.

Armstrong, J. H. *Can Fallen Pastors Be Restored?* Chicago: Moody Press, 1995.

Atkins, D. J., D. F. Field, A. Holmes, and O. O'Donovan. *New Dictionary of Christian Ethics & Pastoral Theology*. Downers Grove, Ill.: InterVarsity Press, 1995.

Bahnsen, G. L. *Homosexuality: a Biblical View*. Grand Rapids: Baker, 1978.

Baker, D. *Beyond Forgiveness*. Portland, Ore.: Multnomah Press, 1984.

———. *Beyond Rejection*. Portland, Ore.: Multnomah Press, 1985.

Barna, G. *Today's Pastors*. Ventura, Calif.: Regal Books, 1993.

Beck, R. N., ed. *Perspectives in Philosophy*. New York: Holt, Rinehart & Winston, 1975.

Berkley, J. D. *Called into Crisis*. Waco: Word, 1989.

Brunner, K. D. *Responsible Living in an Age of Excuses*. Chicago: Moody Press, 1992.

Bullis, R. K., and C. S. Mazur. *Legal Issues and Religious Counseling*. Louisville: Westminster/John Knox Press, 1993.

Carder, D., E. Henslin, J. Townsend, H. Cloud, and A. Brawand. *Secrets of Your Family Tree*. Chicago: Moody Press, 1995.

Christians, C., K. Rotzell, and M. Fackler. *Media Ethics, Cases and Moral Reasoning*. 2d ed. New York: Longman Press, 1990.

Collins, G., ed. *The Secrets of Our Sexuality*. Dallas: Word, 1976.

Dixon, Dr. P. *The Whole Truth about AIDS*. Nashville: Thomas Nelson, 1989.

Dobson, E. G. "Restoring a Fallen Colleague." *Leadership* 13, no. 1 (winter 1992): 106–121.

Editors. "How Common Is Pastoral Indiscretion?" *Leadership* 9, no. 1 (winter 1988): 12–13.

Grollman, E. A. *Suicide: Prevention, Intervention, Postvention*. 2d ed. Boston: Beacon Press, 1988.

Harrison, R. K. *Encyclopedia of Biblical and Christian Ethics*. Nashville: Thomas Nelson, 1987.

Hughes, P. E. *Christian Ethics in Secular Society*. Grand Rapids: Baker, 1983.

Johnson, R. *Your Personality and the Spiritual Life*. Wheaton, Ill.: Victor Books, 1988.

Jordan-Lake, J. "Conduct Unbecoming a Preacher." *Christianity Today* 36, no. 2 (Feb. 10, 1992): 29.

Kantzer, K. S., and C. F. H. Henry, eds. *Evangelical Affirmations*. Grand Rapids: Zondervan, 1990.

Lasch, Christopher. *The Culture of Narcissism.* New York: W. W. Norton & Company, 1978.

Lawrence, W. D. *Beyond the Bottom Line.* Chicago: Moody Press, 1994.

Lewis, H. *A Question of Values.* San Francisco: HarperCollins, 1990.

Merton, T. *Seeds of Contemplation.* New York: New Directions, 1961.

Name Withheld. "Speaking the Truth in Safety." *Leadership* 8, no. 3 (summer 1987): 96–97.

Noyce, G. *Pastoral Ethics: Professional Responsibilities of the Clergy.* Nashville: Abingdon, 1988.

Potter, R. B. *War and Moral Discourse.* Atlanta: John Knox Press, 1969.

Quick, K. "Confidentiality: Will You Tell Overtures?" *Leadership* 12, no. 3 (summer 1991): 103–105.

Sawyer, D. "Polices and Procedures Regarding AIDS." *Leadership* 9, no. 2 (spring 1988): 98.

Shelley, M. *Well-Intentioned Dragons.* Waco: Word, 1985.

Simmons, P. D. *Issues in Christian Ethics.* Nashville: Broadman, 1980.

Spader, D., and G. Mayes. *Growing a Healthy Church.* Chicago: Moody Press, 1991.

Sproul, R. C. *Following Christ.* Wheaton, Ill.: Tyndale House, 1983.

Swindoll, C. R. *Sanctity of Life: The Inescapable Issue.* Dallas: Word, 1990.

Taylor, D. "In Pursuit of Character." *Christianity Today* 39, no. 14 (Dec. 11, 1995): 31.

Teague, W. A. "When a Pastoral Colleague Falls." *Leadership* 12, no. 1 (winter 1991): 102–111.

Trull, J. E., and J. E. Carter. *Ministerial Ethics.* Nashville: Broadman & Holman, 1993.

Van Pelt, R. *Intensive Care: Helping Teenagers in Crisis.* Grand Rapids: Zondervan, 1988.

Walters, C. *Invisible Wounds.* Portland, Ore.: Multnomah Press, 1987.

White, J. *Eros Defiled.* Downers Grove, Ill.: InterVarsity Press, 1977.

Wiest, W. E., and E. A. Smith. *Ethics In Ministry: A Guide for the Professional.* Minneapolis: Fortress Press, 1990.

Worthington, E. L. Jr. *Counseling for Unplanned Pregnancy and Infertility.* Dallas: Word, 1987.

Young, C. *The Least of These.* Chicago: Moody Press, 1984.

FOR FURTHER READING

The following resources are given for additional help, research, and understanding in the area of pastoral ethics and the decision-making process.

Theological Ethics

Anderson, J. *Morality, Law & Grace*. Downers Grove, Ill.: InterVarsity Press, 1972.

Armstrong, John. *Can Fallen Pastors Be Restored?* Chicago: Moody Press, 1995.

Baker, Don. *Beyond Forgiveness*. Portland, Ore.: Multnomah Press, 1984.

Cotham, P. C., ed. *Christian Social Ethics*. Grand Rapids: Baker, 1979.

Erickson, M. J. *Christian Theology*. Grand Rapids: Baker, 1987.

Guthrie, D. *New Testament Theology*. Downers Grove, Ill.: InterVarsity Press, 1981.

Hughes, P. E. *Christian Ethics In Secular Society*. Grand Rapids: Baker, 1983.

Kantzer, K. S., and C. F. H. Henry, eds. *Evangelical Affirmations*. Grand Rapids: Zondervan, 1990.

Layman, S. *The Shape of the Good*. South Bend, Ind.: University of Notre Dame Press, 1991.

Mouw, R. *The God Who Commands*. South Bend, Ind.: University of Notre Dame Press, 1991.

Smedes, L. *A Pretty Good Person*. San Francisco: Harper & Row, 1991.

———. *Choices: Making Right Decisions in a Complex World*. San Francisco: Harper & Row, 1986.

———. *Forgive and Forget*. San Francisco: Harper & Row, 1984.

———. *Love within Limits*. Grand Rapids: Eerdmans, 1982.

———. *Mere Morality*. Grand Rapids: Eerdmans, 1983.

Sproul, R. C. *Following Christ*. Wheaton, Ill.: Tyndale House, 1983.

Moral Theory and Decision Making

Bok, S. *Lying: Moral Choice in Public and Private Life*. New York: Vintage Books, 1989.

———. *Secrets*. New York: Pantheon Books, 1982.

Bullis, R. K., and C. S. Mazur. *Legal Issues and Religious Counseling*. Louisville: Westminster/John Knox, 1993.

Bowie, N. E. *Making Ethical Decisions*. New York: McGraw-Hill, 1985.

Christians, C., K. Rotzoll, and M. Fackler. *Media Ethics: Cases and Moral Reasoning*. 2d ed. New York: Longman Press, 1987.

Clark, R. W. *Introduction to Moral Reasoning*. New York: West, 1986.

Davis, J. J. *Evangelical Ethics*. Phillipsburg, Pa.: Presbyterian & Reformed, 1985.

Deats, P. Jr., ed. *Toward a Discipline of Social Ethics*. Boston: Boston University Press, 1972.

Fosdick, H. E. *Twelve Tests of Character*. London: Student Christian Movement, 1924.

Geisler, N. B. *Ethics, Alternatives and Issues*. Grand Rapids: Eerdmans, 1971.

Holmes, A. F. *Ethics: Approaching Moral Decisions*. Downers Grove, Ill.: InterVarsity Press, 1984.

————. *Shaping Character*. Grand Rapids: Eerdmans, 1990.

House, W. H. *Christian Ministries and the Law*. Grand Rapids: Baker, 1992.

Lewis, H. *A Question of Values*. New York: Harper & Row, 1990.

Lebacqz, K. *Professional Ethics: Power and Paradox*. Nashville: Abingdon, 1985.

Murray, H. L. *Changing Expectations and Ethics in the Professional Ministry*. Evanston, Ill.: Garret Theological Seminary Press, 1969.

Mueller, F. *Ethical Dilemma of Ministers*. London: C. Scribner & Sons, 1937.

Noyce, G., *Pastoral Ethics*. Nashville: Abingdon, 1988.

Stob, H. *Ethical Reflections: Essays on Moral Themes*. Grand Rapids: Eerdmans, 1978.

Trull, J. E., and J. E. Carter. *Ministerial Ethics*. Nashville: Broadman and Holman, 1993.

Wiest, W. E., and E. A. Smith. *Ethics in Ministry*. Minneapolis: Fortress, 1990.

Articles

Bok, S. "The Limits of Confidentiality," Hastings Center Report, February 1983.

Quick, K. "Confidentiality: Will You Tell Overtures?" *Leadership* 12, no. 3 (summer 1991).

Sawyer, D. "Polices and Procedures Regarding AIDS." *Leadership* 9, no. 2 (spring 1988).